LEARNING HOW TO SAY NO WHEN YOU USUALLY SAY YES

Everything You Need to Know Explained Simply

MARITZA B. MANRESA

Learning How to Say No When You Usually Say Yes: Everything You Need to Know Explained Simply

Copyright © 2012 by Atlantic Publishing Group, Inc.
1405 SW 6th Ave. • Ocala, Florida 34471 • 800-814-1132 • 352-622-1875–Fax
Website: www.atlantic-pub.com • E-mail: sales@atlantic-pub.com
SAN Number: 268-1250

Library of Congress Cataloging-in-Publication Data

Manresa, Maritza B., 1965-
  Learning how to say no when you usually say yes : everything you need to know explained simply / by Maritza B. Manresa.
      p. cm.
  Includes bibliographical references and index.
  ISBN-13: 978-1-60138-384-6 (alk. paper)
  ISBN-10: 1-60138-384-3 (alk. paper)
  1. Assertiveness (Psychology) 2. Acquiescence (Psychology) 3. Control (Psychology) 4. Change (Psychology) I. Title.
  BF575.A85M26 2011
  158.2--dc22
                                    2011012925

Printed in the United States

Printed on Recycled Paper

PROJECT MANAGER: Amy Moczynski • ASSISTANT EDITOR: Angela Pham
BOOK PRODUCTION DESIGN: T.L. Price • design@tlpricefreelance.com
PROOFREADER: C&P Marse • bluemoon6749@bellsouth.net
FRONT/BACK COVER DESIGN: Jackie Miller • millerjackiej@gmail.com

A few years back we lost our beloved pet dog Bear, who was not only our best and dearest friend but also the "Vice President of Sunshine" here at Atlantic Publishing. He did not receive a salary but worked tirelessly 24 hours a day to please his parents.

Bear was a rescue dog who turned around and showered myself, my wife, Sherri, his grandparents Jean, Bob, and Nancy, and every person and animal he met (well, maybe not rabbits) with friendship and love. He made a lot of people smile every day.

We wanted you to know a portion of the profits of this book will be donated in Bear's memory to local animal shelters, parks, conservation organizations, and other individuals and nonprofit organizations in need of assistance.

– Douglas & Sherri Brown

PS: We have since adopted two more rescue dogs: first Scout, and the following year, Ginger. They were both mixed golden retrievers who needed a home.

Want to help animals and the world? Here are a dozen easy suggestions you and your family can implement today:

- *Adopt and rescue a pet from a local shelter.*
- *Support local and no-kill animal shelters.*
- *Plant a tree to honor someone you love.*
- *Be a developer — put up some birdhouses.*
- *Buy live, potted Christmas trees and replant them.*
- *Make sure you spend time with your animals each day.*
- *Save natural resources by recycling and buying recycled products.*
- *Drink tap water, or filter your own water at home.*
- *Whenever possible, limit your use of or do not use pesticides.*
- *If you eat seafood, make sustainable choices.*
- *Support your local farmers market.*
- *Get outside. Visit a park, volunteer, walk your dog, or ride your bike.*

Five years ago, Atlantic Publishing signed the Green Press Initiative. These guidelines promote environmentally friendly practices, such as using recycled stock and vegetable-based inks, avoiding waste, choosing energy-efficient resources, and promoting a no-pulping policy. We now use 100-percent recycled stock on all our books. The results: in one year, switching to post-consumer recycled stock saved 24 mature trees, 5,000 gallons of water, the equivalent of the total energy used for one home in a year, and the equivalent of the greenhouse gases from one car driven for a year.

DEDICATION

With much love and appreciation to my husband,
Manny, and my children, Wesley and Monica,
for their encouragement, love, and support.

AUTHOR ACKNOWLEDGMENTS

Writing this book, as well as my previous book, was a task I did not take lightly. I felt a great deal of responsibility for what was about to be published as people, hopefully, would be using the information provided to better themselves. For that reason, I dedicated a great deal of time and effort in making sure the information was well researched and accurate.

In the process of putting this book together, a lot of great people were instrumental in making it the fabulous book that it turned out to be. I would like to first thank the case study participants who, through their participation, allowed me to peek into other people's experiences with their struggle to say No when they know they should say No. Their candid answers made me realize what a common struggle saying No is for so many people and from so many different walks of life.

I could not miss this opportunity to thank all my longtime friends and new friends who have walked with me through this journey of completing this book, offering me their constant love, support, and, most of all, words of encouragement. To my friends and sisters at the Tree of Life who have taught me so much about the power we all have within us to make things possible I say, keep manifesting because anything is possible!

I have to thank my family – my brother, Julio, who is my strength, always holding my hand through calm and stormy weather, and my sister, Martha. My parents, Martha and Julio, who have always been so proud of me, and have always encouraged me to reach for the stars because they are mine for the taking, if I want them bad enough. They taught me that there are no limits to what I can accomplish if I set my mind to it, and so I have.

Most important, I would like to thank my husband, Manny, and my children, Wesley and Monica. My children — what a precious gift! Their love, support, and encouragement to pursue my dreams was always ever so present. Their pride and belief in me kept me going even during the hardest times. My husband, for always being there by my side and being my "biggest fan," and for providing me with the opportunity to follow my dreams and work on what I really love to do — to write.

Chapter Five: Saying No To Friends 81

Chapter Six: Saying No To Family.....101

Chapter Eleven: What About Those Times You Must Say Yes? 237

SO OFTEN WE FIND OURSELVES IN SITUATIONS WHERE our mouths are saying Yes to something while our brains are screaming, "Say no. You cannot do this. You don't have time to handle one more thing!" But we go ahead and commit to take care of that one more thing. To some people, this is not a common everyday occurrence, but for others, this seems to be their way of life. If you have a hard time saying No to people, you more than likely are a "giver." You are someone who has a great heart but not-so-great assertiveness skills. You would take the shirt off your back to give it to someone else, even though you might need it. If this is you we are talking about, then this book is for you.

It is my intention for this book to be an eye-opener and become your guide by assisting you as you commence your journey into your new life of freedom from the burden you have created by always saying Yes. When we are constantly agreeing to do things for other people, we are taking up time we could be using on things we really want to do. We get so caught up in trying to please others and to be such good stewards to humanity that we forget to take ourselves — our needs — into consideration. We take on so much that we end up losing control of our lives and turn them in to total chaos because we end up having to be here and there at the same time. So not only do we end up getting mad at ourselves for having said Yes one more time, but we also tend to get mad at the person who asked us to perform said task. It is not their fault we said Yes. Although we may come up with all kinds of reasons and justifications as to why we should be agreeing to do things we do not really want to do, the reality is that we need to start coming up with reasons and justifications as to why we should be saying No to those requests.

A good start is to start saying No to small things — situations and requests you might deal with on a daily basis with family, friends, or coworkers that will not take too much more effort to say No. Just as there are times when we finally blow up out of frustration because we have been holding on to a number of small things that bother us, the same holds true for saying Yes more often than we should. Too many Yeses can generate an overwhelming feeling, which eventually takes a toll on us.

You should always be No. 1 priority in your life because if your needs are not met, you will not be able to effectively meet the needs of those around you. That is why it is so important that we learn to say No when we really mean No and learn how to chose the situations in which we want to say Yes. That is what this book will do for you.

However, before you can learn how to say No effectively and convincingly, it is important to first truly understand why is it that we tend to say Yes. The first portion of the book will help you identify the reasons why you will usually say Yes when you should be saying No. When you start looking at the many reasons why you have been saying Yes, you will soon realize that most of the times, your response is more the result of a subconscious decision rather than a rational decision.

Subconscious decisions are decisions based on learned patterns of behavior that you have been conditioned to from childhood that are difficult, but not impossible, to overcome. Often these decisions are based on the premise of "what will people think." We are always so worried about what people think of us. We want so badly for people to think nothing but great things about us that we overextend ourselves in the process. The feeling of wanting to belong and be accepted is just human nature. The need to be accepted has been actually categorized as one of the basic human needs based on a study conducted in 1943 by Abraham Maslow, which will be addressed in more detail in Chapter 4.

Therefore, you say Yes to oversee a committee in the club you belong to, and you agree to organize the upcoming charity event on top of already having agreed to be the den mother of your son's Cub Scouts troop or coaching your daughter's soccer team. In addition to all that, you want to be a good son or daughter, a good friend, and a good employee, so you agree to numerous requests by your mother to take her shopping. You agree to take your friend to a specialist doctor out of town, while at the same time, you take on extra responsibilities at work that result in our getting home late a couple of times a week. Still, it does not end there. Aside from all the added responsibilities that have resulted from all your Yeses, you still have all your other everyday responsibilities that need to be taken care of as well.

The book will discuss saying No to family, friends, and in the workplace. You are probably thinking, "Saying No to my mother, or my best friend, worst yet, saying No to my boss? Don't think it's possible." Well, it is not only possible, but it is possible to do this and feel free from guilt. We will discuss a multiple array of situations in which you do not really need to respond Yes or No, but rather situations in which your lack of response is perceived as a Yes. You may not necessarily have to respond with a No in these situations, but your actions say it for you.

You are going to be working toward creating a new you — a new, assertive you who is not afraid to say No or worry about what people are going to think because you said No. You are going to learn how to set some boundaries and give yourself the place you deserve, which is right on top of the "totem pole." People will respect you for who you are. You will feel better and more confident knowing that the people who really care about you will understand that sometimes you just have to say No. Those around you will understand it is nothing personal, but it is something you must do at that particular moment in time. When you start saying No with confidence, and without hesitation, to requests that you know deep in your heart you simply cannot tackle or really do not want to take care of, you are going to wish you had started on that path much earlier.

However, saying No is not only a choice you make in everyday situations, it is also a choice you might have to make in not-so-common circumstances, such as abusive relationships or compromising requests. Hopefully you will never find yourself in such situations, but should you, maybe having given it some thought ahead of time will help you through it.

Most of the time, using common sense and being levelheaded in difficult situations can make a difference between being able to successfully get out of the situation or just giving in. Although simply saying No might not be the answer in difficult circumstances, the actions you take, or do not take, will have a great effect on the outcome of such situations. Always remember the old wise saying that actions speak louder than words. Your reaction stating an explicit, nonverbal No will have as much of an impact, if not more, than a No spoken out loud.

Most important, remember that you are not alone. More people out there in the world do not know how to say No than those who have actually mastered the art of saying No. For that matter, while working on this book, any time

I mentioned I was working on a book about learning how to say No, every single person made some type of comment on how much they needed to learn that trait. They would further elaborate on how many times they end up saying Yes when they know they should be saying No and the consequences that followed such deeds.

I am convinced that, in one way or another, we all need help learning how to say No. Some people may be strong enough individuals that they very seldom give in to feelings of obligation or guilt and instead remain true to their convictions by saying No when they know that is the appropriate answer. But, for those few times when they have weakened, a good boost from a book like this never hurts. Nevertheless, for those true "Yesaholics," there is a lot of information that will certainly help with your "Yes addiction."

In addition to several case studies included in the book about real people who have learned, or are learning, to set boundaries that allow them to say No, you will also find throughout the book what I have called "Confessions of a Yesaholic." These "confessions" are examples from real people about real life situations they have encountered and how they have handled them. Some have been able to say No when they would have normally said Yes, and some have said Yes to situations they should have said No to and then had to deal with the consequences.

It is not easy for anyone to change the way he or she has always done things because that is what we feel comfortable with. We are creatures of habit and naturally afraid of the unknown. Changing from being a "Yes person" to a person who can effectively say No requires making a serious evaluation of what causes us to behave this way. Once we understand what it is that makes us act one way or another, then it makes it easier to find a solution and change the way we function. We have to come to terms with the fact that we have a problem before we can try to find a solution, and once we have accomplished that, we can then move forward. The important thing is that you are ready to make changes to take control of your life and pursue your happiness.

Wondering if people around you will approve or disapprove should not make you question whether you want to take this leap of faith, because the answer is Yes. You want to make this change because it is for your own good and the good of those closest to you. It will actually have a positive ripple effect that will expand beyond your reach. As with any other habit, change is not going to happen overnight, but with faith in yourself and lots of perseverance, you will accomplish it. By picking up this book, you have taken a step in the right direction, and soon you will be well on your way to a more productive, happier, and self-fulfilling life.

why you say yes when you mean no

"WHY DID I SAY YES WHEN I REALLY WANTED TO SAY No?" You probably ask yourself this question every time you agree to another task, and yet, you continue to do it. The answer is not straightforward, as it probably is a combination of issues and circumstances that lead you to such behavior — behavior that can be changed. It is not all about changing who you are and turning into a self-centered individual who says No to every request is made of you. It is all about balance — sometimes saying Yes and sometimes saying No. Sometimes people say Yes because it gives them a sense of fulfillment of having helped others, and everyone needs some of that. People also help others in the hopes that one day when they need help and ask a friend for a favor, their friend will say Yes. It is about giving and receiving. But you must be careful about how often you are saying Yes because that wonderful feeling you get from helping others soon is replaced by a feeling of anxiety and desperation because helping others has put you in a bind.

As a norm, when someone approaches with a request, most of the time the answer you give people in that situation, whether it is a Yes or No answer, depends on the circumstances surrounding that one particular setting. Further, when you answer Yes to someone's request when you know you should have answered No, the reason for such a response can be more of a psychological nature rather than totally circumstantial. In those instances, you are responding based on embedded early childhood conditioning, such as fear of being disliked, fear of challenging authority, out of a sense of responsibility, or even lack of self-confidence.

You Say Yes Because... That Is What You Were Taught

One of the most common reasons you say Yes when you should be saying No is the result of early childhood cultural conditioning that taught you that answering people's requests with a No is not being polite. Starting at a young age, children learn the importance of being polite, and one way of being polite is to say Yes when people ask you to do something for them. Children learn to always help those who cannot do for themselves and that they should always help the elderly and disabled, as well as those who are less fortunate. Unfortunately, this creates an unhealthy psychological pattern that many still practice as adults. These habits often create the inability to say No, even when you absolutely cannot comply, when it relates to people who would fall under such categories. Take for instance the time when as a child, you were out riding your bicycle with your friends, and your mother interrupted your playtime to ask you to go bring the groceries in for your elderly neighbor. You wanted to say No because you were playing, but your mother was teaching you a life lesson about being polite — helping your neighbor. Also, you were following the rules and being obedient toward adults. Though that was an important lesson for a child to learn, that instance played a role in your conditioning as a child. Aside from being obedient and helping the elderly, you were being "programmed" to put the needs of others before your needs.

As you got older, you continued to follow the pattern that your parents taught you, thereby creating the habit of always telling people Yes when they asked something of you because it was the polite thing to do. So, now as an adult you say Yes to just about everything and anyone because that is what you were taught to do, regardless of how overwhelmed you may feel. However, as important as being polite might be, doing everything to extremes is not healthy. There has to be a balance between being polite and knowing when to say No. As a child, being polite and helping others took priority over other things. However, now as an adult, life is different and priorities have changed. You now have other responsibilities, and as much as you want to help others in need, you must take your own needs and responsibilities into account before taking on additional tasks. Regardless of what you might have been taught, you can say No to people — in a nice way, that is — and still be polite.

CASE STUDY:
THE REV. VICKIE HAREN

Certified Spiritual Life Coach
Lady Lake, Florida

Until recent years, the Rev. Haren was conditioned to say Yes to everything since she was a child because as she explains it, "I was born the oldest daughter in my family. My 'job' was to take care of the house when my mother was away at work. The harder I worked, the more praise I received. I was hooked on what others thought of me, and their praise gave me wonderful energy."

In the past, the word No was not in the Rev. Haren's vocabulary. She could do it all and, most of all, loved it when people would comment on how much work she could handle, which was a reflection of her upbringing. Then, she began to understand how she was losing herself in the process and could feel inner tension when she did not succeed in doing all she had promised to do. This tension resulted in tremendous stress, which she noticed was being reflected in physical ailments in her body on her shoulders and neck area. So, she began to pay more attention to her body, specifically how it felt in any given situation.

One of her earliest recollections of having to learn to say No goes back several years ago to the times when she owed a small manufacturing business in Ohio. She employed several women, most of whom were her friends. Each of these friends had an opinion on how to improve her business, and rather than saying Yes to some and No to others, she found herself going crazy trying to implement all of their ideas. It was at that moment that she understood she was going to have to say No to someone, so she decided to do what she thought would be best for her business, rather than doing what everyone else was suggesting.

Now, taking time to consider the request being made of her before answering has allowed her to feel more comfortable with her final decision when she answers Yes or No. Her realizing that she must be sure she is fully capable of taking care of the task has made a great difference. Because as she explains it, "I can't give away what I don't have."

Another one of those important behaviors you were taught from childhood was that of reciprocating favors. You are taught that if others do something nice for you, you should do something nice for them. Undoubtedly, it is a very important life lesson, but sometimes it can come back to haunt you at the most inopportune circumstances.

For instance, say that two months ago you and your spouse were going to a concert. You had purchased the tickets ahead of time and were planning a night out. The day of the concert, your babysitter calls and tells you that she has a date that night and will not be able to babysit. You are stuck; not only is the concert a one-time event, but you paid a small fortune for those tickets, so you most definitely want to go. As you scramble to find a solution, you think of your friend Jessie, you call her up, and she agrees to babysit. Today, Jessie calls you and tells you she needs you to take care of her children tonight because of a last-minute outing with her spouse. Regardless of the fact that you were planning a night out with your girlfriends, you drop everything and agree to babysit. However, because somehow people always feel the need of not being indebted to anybody, they tend to do more than they were asked to do, so not only do you agree to babysit them, you volunteer to keep them until the following day so they do not have to rush back. Not only did you feel you had to pay back her previous favor, but subconsciously you wanted to make sure you were one up on her. This does not mean that next time she asks you for a favor you are going to say No. More than likely, you would have said Yes because of your feeling of owing her for some previous favor she might have done for you (even if you cannot remember what that favor might have been). Notice the phrasing "would have said," because that is the very intention of this book, changing your "will say Yes," to "would have said" because you no longer will be saying Yes under those circumstances.

At times, you might even say Yes as a feeling of reciprocation — not because of a specific favor you want to pay back, but because sometimes in long-term relationships people are reminded of the things their partner has done for them in the past, thereby creating a sense of indebtedness. It can be as subtle as in regular conversation with your friend reminiscing of how she used to cover up for you when you skipped class in high school, or how she would always drive you where you needed to go when you did not have a car, or how many times she loaned you money when you were running short. The list goes on. You are never able to put all those favors in the past and, although she might have not done anything for you in the past ten years, you are still going to feel like you need to reciprocate by saying Yes every time she asks something of you. This cycle is not easy to break because we are highly trained in reciprocating. For instance, someone gives you a gift, and you immediately feel like you have to give him or her one back (it is kind of expected). What about carpooling? It is the old "You scratch my back; I scratch yours" concept. Reciprocating is not a bad thing when the parties involved have mutual understanding and when it is practiced within reason. However, the problem with reciprocating is that much too often people find themselves saying Yes even when they know it should have been absolutely No. At some point, saying Yes because you feel you have to reciprocate favors has to come to a stop, and your Yeses should be out of "wanting to" not "having to."

Growing up, one of the biggest and most important lessons to learn was that of getting along with others. Parents and teachers tell children that if they wanted to get anywhere in life, they had to learn to get along with others, which sometimes really translated into going along and not creating any ripples in the water. The problem with this concept is that in the effort to get along with others, many people often find themselves saying Yes to people when they know deep down they should be saying No. It is natural to want to get along with others and avoid confrontations at all costs, which means that in order to avoid confrontations, often people feel they need to compromise and say Yes, even when they know it is going to cause hardships.

A Yesaholic confesses: "*Every year for Thanksgiving, my family (husband and children) always have Thanksgiving at my parents' house because my brothers and sisters always gather there for a big family outing. However, this year my husband proposed that instead of going to my parents', we should go away to the mountains on holiday for that week and have cozy Thanksgiving just us and the kids. It really sounded like fun, and it would have been something different. The kids were excited, and I was seriously thinking about going with that plan. That was until my mother called with my dish assignment for the Thanksgiving feast because she was assuming we would be there as we always have been. I started to hesitate and then she popped the question, 'You are not thinking about going somewhere else are you? You are going to be here, right?' So what did I do? I said 'Yes, mother, of course, we will be there.' I had to say Yes because I did not want to create any issues in our family; I just want to get along with everyone as I was always taught. I ended up spending Thanksgiving with the family; however, while we were all together that day, I took the opportunity to announce that the following year we would not join the rest of the family for Thanksgiving because we were going to be away for the holiday. I figured that way I would avoid having* to say *No* to mother next year when she called to arrange for the holiday dinner. Speaking up ahead of time saved me the process of agonizing over having to say *No* to something I was expected to comply with and made me feel empowered and in control of my own life."

The conditioning you experience from childhood brings you into adulthood with a lot of baggage. You find yourself constantly saying Yes to people regardless of what you really want because of that deep-rooted sense of having to be polite, to reciprocate favors, and to get along with others. Not being able to overcome these feelings can cause you to feel guilty when you say No to somebody. However, it is essential to understand that the guilt you experience is completely unfounded, and you must learn to overcome such feelings, thereby allowing you to feel confident and guilt free whenever you say No. The purpose of this information is by no means a way of raising red flags with you or making you feel as if you were brought up the wrong way. It is only intended to help you realize why it is that you usually say Yes when you should be saying No, and hopefully this will be an eye opener that will help you make that transition to learning how to effectively say No. It is only by coming to terms with weaknesses that you are able to overcome them.

You Say Yes Because...
You Want to be Liked by All

This is a big one — everyone wants to be liked. You want to be liked by your parents, friends, peers, boss, coworkers, you name it. You meet people and you immediately strive to make a good first impression because you want to be liked. However, as important as it is to everybody to be liked, it is more important to take into consideration what is good for you rather than worrying about what other people think of you. Often, you find yourself in a bind because someone asks you to take care of something for him or her, and because you are so worried about what they will think if you say No, you quickly respond Yes, regardless of the request or your real ability to comply.

Sometimes people you barely know make these requests.

For instance, say you just moved your kids to a new school that has annual carnivals as fundraisers. The chairwoman of the school carnival committee is looking for volunteers and has asked you to run the marketing committee. You are a terribly shy person, and you know that this is almost an impossible task for you to accomplish, but because you want to be liked and you do not want the other parents at school gossiping about how you did not take on the "simple" task that was asked of you, you accept. You are now not only faced with a task at hand that you probably do not really have the time to spare to handle, but you also are taking care of something you have a hard time dealing with. On the bright side, you may try to use this project as a way to try to overcome your shyness, but that is something that should be done gradually and not during a one-time opportunity. The problem with jumping into a Yes because you want to be liked in a situation such as this is that you may end up doing a poor job because marketing and public relations are just not your strong suits. So what happens? You said Yes to the request in an effort to be liked by others, but you ended up being disliked even more because you failed to perform as expected, thereby defeating the purpose of why you accepted the task in the first place.

There are even times when people fall for flattery and say Yes. Who does not like to hear all about how great and wonderful they are? Everyone does, especially because being flattered is supposed to be testament to just how much that particular person likes you. So, how can you disappoint someone who has just made you feel so well liked and so great about yourself by saying No to them? Well, unfortunately, flattery does not always come from the heart, and, at times, it may be delivered with a hidden agenda. Just like there are people out there who find all kinds of reasons why they should say Yes to others, there are people out there who will avail themselves of whatever they can to have people do things for them. Flattery always gives you such a boost of self-esteem and energy that makes you feel like you can really go out there and tackle the world. Well-intended and sincere flattery is always welcomed, but it is not much of a compliment when it has been done with ulterior motives.

For instance, James is an excellent writer, and he really enjoys writing at his leisure. James has published several articles in a local magazine, which gives him a little bit of exposure. Besides his writing, he is also a full-time employee with a very hectic life. Then, the chairwoman of a local charity for which he volunteers becomes aware of his writing skills and decides to tap into James' talent. The next time James sees her in a public setting, she boasts about his writing abilities, commends James on his writing skills, and proceeds to ask if he would be willing to put his talent to work for the charitable organization. She then asks James to write the organization's monthly newsletter. In this case, flattery was only a means of getting on James' good side so he would feel obliged to accept her request. Therefore, becoming aware of such situations is just one of the steps you will be taking toward learning how to say No when you would otherwise say Yes.

You Say Yes Because... You Do Not Want to Challenge Authority

How many times has your boss asked you to stay late to finish a project or take work home over the weekend when you know doing so will conflict with your plans? Probably more often than you care to remember, especially when your answer to those requests were Yes because you did not want to challenge authority or displease your employer. Both of these reasons are rooted in your desire to retain your employment.

Although not limited to the workplace, this situation is most prevalent in boss/employee situations. There is no question that in any work environment there is always a boss (at least one) and there are the employees.

Therefore, from the moment employees are hired for a position, they strive to do their best to keep the boss happy and satisfied with their performance. They do not challenge his or her authority because he or she is in charge. However, bosses are just people, and at times, when bosses get overwhelmed with work, they tend to pass this on down to the employees, demanding more of them and, at times, making unreasonable requests. Other bosses, because of their positions of power, adopt a sense of greatness and expect their employees to comply with every one of their requests simply because they are the bosses. Then there are bosses who continue to assign their employees new tasks because they do not realize that these employees already have a great deal to accomplish. Regardless of what the reason is for your boss to continue to make unreasonable requests, you have the right to say No respectfully and without challenging his/her authority.

You will encounter many other situations from time to time when you are drawn to say Yes rather than No because the person making the request is an authority figure. Watch out also for people in your community who are authority figures and make requests to which you know the answer should be a resounding No, but because they are an authority figure, you buckle and say Yes.

For example, you live in a relatively small town, and you run a tax preparation and notary public business from within an accountant's offices. For some reason, the city government had to vote on a land-use change to allow for your business to operate out of the accountant's office, and during the voting, Mr. Jackson, the city commission's president, cast an affirmative vote that broke the tie, thereby allowing you to open your business. A year later, Mr. Jackson comes by your office with a legal document asking you to notarize his signature and his wife's signature. The only problem is that his wife's signature is already on the document, and she is not there to attest to her signature. You tell Mr. Jackson that you cannot notarize the wife's signature because she did not sign in your presence and thereby you would be notarizing said

> *document illegally. At that point, Mr. Jackson proceeds to remind you how his vote allowed you to open your business and that he thinks you owe him one. What do you do? Legally you should say No. However, because he is such an authority figure, and his actions could at some point have an influence in your business, more than likely you would be inclined to say Yes.*

So, how do you go from feeling inclined to say Yes to actually saying No in a situation like this? You arm yourself with confidence and courage, knowing that you cannot go wrong when you do things ethically and legally, and you proceed to tell Mr. Jackson that you cannot notarize the document for him. You let him know how much you really appreciate what he has done for you in the past, but legally you cannot notarize the document, and you do not want to risk losing your license over this.

You Say Yes Because... You Feel You Have to Say Yes

Having a sense of responsibility is a good and honorable trait. Unfortunately, a number of people in the world today are self-centered and could not care less how their actions will affect others, but there are others who still act guided by a well-founded sense of responsibility and always try to do the right thing. However, sometimes in an effort to always do what is right, people can get caught up in the loop of always saying Yes, even at times when they should be saying No. For example, you may feel that it is your responsibility as the oldest sibling to see to it that family traditions are continued after your parents can no longer continue to organize or carry out these outings. So, you end up taking charge of each of the family events just to make sure they happen. Charging ahead and taking charge of a task is saying Yes, even if you have not used spoken words to state so. What happens is that because of that sense of responsibility, you may have taken on more than what you could possibly handle. What you fail to see is that it is not solely your responsibility and other members of the family may be willing to chip in should you ask for the help.

At times, you may even say Yes, not because you want to do something, but because you feel obliged to comply.

For instance, Tim is a college student not living too far away from home. His mother calls and tells him that she would like for him to come home this weekend because his second cousin Tammy whom he has not seen since they were kids is coming to town this weekend, and she is having a dinner party. The problem is that Tim has a major paper due that Monday that will count for half of his grade, and he has not even started on it. So Tim tells his mother that he does not think he will be able to attend; however, Tim's mother proceeds to tell him how he will be the only one not there and how

> disappointed cousin Tammy will be if he does not show up. What did he do? Tim ended up saying Yes because he felt obliged to attend. As a result, he ended up staying up all night the night before the paper was due because he took valuable time that he could have invested in his paper and attended a family function to which he should have said "No, I will see her some other time."

In the future, Tim needs to assert himself and, regardless of how hard his mother tries to make him feel guilty, he needs to state his reasons for not being able to attend and take care of his school paper instead.

You Say Yes Because... You Do Not Have the Courage to Say No

Not being assertive is one of the reasons why people let that Yes come out of their mouths when their insides are yelling, "Say No!" The bottom line is that you are not assertive enough to muster up the courage to say No. Although you might mentally go through the process of evaluating why you should say No, such as knowing it is because of some hang-up from childhood, or because you just lack the assertiveness in your actions, you still mgiht end up saying Yes. People seem to lack assertiveness because of low self-esteem issues and not having enough confidence in themselves. It is almost a feeling of being unworthy of standing up for what they believe and for who they are, so people say Yes to please others, to accommodate others, to make others feel important, or for whatever other reason other than for what is important to them.

For instance, how often do you say Yes by not stating your wishes, and you let someone else decide for you? That is saying Yes to whatever decision is being made when you could be voicing your opinion saying No. For example, you are part of the committee planning the company picnic, and as the chairman goes around the table making assignments as to who is going to be heading which subcommittee, you are assigned the food committee. You do not want to head this committee because you cannot commit to any more than you already have. However, instead of saying "No, I cannot take on that new task," you stay quiet, thereby stating a silent Yes.

When you allow yourself to say Yes at times when you should be saying No, subconsciously, you are taking the position that the needs of the person who asked you are more important than your own. You are thinking about how badly that person needs your help or how much more important their need is than yours, so you must offer support. Or perhaps you are thinking that they are so much older and not as able as you are, so you must say Yes. However, what about you? Regardless of position within social stratification, age, or anything else, you must remember that you are just as important as anyone else. Your needs, desires, and interests must be taken into account as well as everybody else's. When you lack the assertiveness that you need to be able to say No when you should, you tend to say Yes to people you feel are like you. Because of this commonality, you feel a bond brings you together, and so you must support each other and be there for each other in times of need. Unfortunately, in most situations like these, there is always one party that does most of the helping, saying Yes, while the other one does the asking. Thereby, this relationship that is perceived to be a "help each other" relationship ends up being mostly one-sided.

The fact that you usually say Yes when you should be saying No is not to be taken lightly. The consequences of your inability to say No may be as simple as a minor inconvenience to you in the lend, or they can be as severe as actually costing you money.

> For example, think about a small business owner who specializes in fence installation. He submits a proposal to his clients that upon signature becomes a binding contract for the work. However, halfway through the project, the property owner requests the fence contractor to build a dog kennel right away because his wife adopted two large dogs, and she will be bringing them home in the next two to three days. Wanting to keep the customer satisfied, and in light of the apparent emergency, the contractor says Yes and proceeds to

build the kennel instead of saying, "No, I need to amend the current contract or write a new contract for the kennel before I can proceed." Unfortunately for the subcontractor, he has run into a dishonest homeowner who then decides when the work is complete not to pay for the kennel because there was not a contract for such work. In a case like this, a simple No followed by the appropriate action to proceed with the work would have saved the contractor time and money.

As you can see, people say Yes when they should say No for many different reasons, and what might seem like a good reason for one person to say Yes to a specific request may not be the same reason for someone else. Going back and evaluating why you said Yes in a particular instance when you know you should have said No will serve as great tool in helping you make the right decision when you are faced with the same or a similar situation in the future.

You want to make sure that you say No, or Yes, at the appropriate times so you can learn to create a balance in your life. When you get in the habit of saying Yes to accommodate everyone else's needs rather than taking yourself into consideration and worrying about your own needs, you will soon get overwhelmed and frustrated. You are as important as everyone else, which gives you the right to say No when you need to do so.

CHAPTER TWO

you have the right to say no

OF COURSE, YOU HAVE THE RIGHT TO SAY NO AT ANY time you do not feel comfortable saying Yes to any one request. You are the author of your life, and you write your own life's story, which means you have total power to make decisions that affect you as a person and how your proceed in life, in general. Regardless of what you think other people's expectations of you may be, what is important is what you ultimately expect of yourself. Constantly saying Yes and fulfilling everybody else's expectations may be keeping you from achieving your own expectations, thereby creating within yourself a feeling of dissatisfaction and low self-worth for not being able to do all that you really wanted to do.

You Are the No. I Priority in Your Life, Learn to Say No

If you are usually saying Yes to others without thinking through it or evaluating how this Yes may affect you, it is definitely a sign that you are putting others' interests ahead of yours. Doing this on a regular basis is not mentally or physically healthy for you. Before answering Yes to any request, especially if you know it is going to be something that will require a great deal of time and effort on your part, you should take a moment and evaluate whether agreeing to such a request is really what you want to do. Is saying Yes to others translating into saying No to those things that are important to you? Learning how to say No will make you feel more confident and in control of your life. Before you say Yes to any requests, ask yourself first if this is something you really want to do. If the answer is No, then your response should be No as well. Is going to your boss's daughter's volleyball game more important than going home to your children whom you have not seen all day? The answer should be No. So, when your boss tells you and the other employees in the office that his daughter, who is such a great volleyball player, is having a game that afternoon, and he would like for you to go, your response should be that you are sure his daughter is going to do a great job; you would love to see her play, but that you already have other plans for the evening, and maybe next time you can go. Do not let the pressure of your boss asking you for something that is not work-related take priority over what is important to you. The fact that you did not attend his daughter's volleyball game should not have any bearing when it comes to evaluating your job performance.

Also, do not agree to things out of guilt. You may agree with a request because you think you will feel guilty if you do not follow through with the request, but the truth is that, in the end, the only guilt you are going to feel is that of not having said No. That is because you agreed to something you really did not want to do. Acting out of guilt does not necessarily have to be related to one single event. Sometimes, the accumulation of small issues create a big one.

For instance, your church is taking a mission trip to a very poor community out of the country, and you have been asked to participate. Not only will you be contributing with your talents as a construction contractor, but also you will also be responsible for all your expenses. The trip is expected to last two weeks during the summer, and although you would like to participate, you had made tentative plans to go on vacation to Mexico with your family on one of those two weeks. You know you cannot afford both trips, not only financially, but also time-wise. As a small business owner, you cannot afford to be gone that long during the summer months. So, you tell the mission trip coordinators that you cannot participate because you have other plans. However, they continue to insist that there are no other contractors available to go and that because you have been so blessed financially that you should give to those less fortunate. They even suggest that you postpone your family vacation and go during the

> *Christmas holiday. You start feeling so guilty that you actually consider saying Yes to the mission trip and postponing your family vacation. However, as you move closer to making a final decision, you realize that you are saying Yes to the mission trip out of guilt, not because you heart is in it at this point. You realize that there will be other opportunities to participate on mission trips and decide to go on your family vacation, which you all need and deserve.*

Saying Yes out of guilt sometimes could be the result of a more deep-rooted problem. When this is the case, people tend to say Yes blindly without thinking about the consequences of their inability to say No when it is unreasonable to say Yes one more time. One good example of such a situation is that of divorced parents with their children. Anybody who has been in this situation is familiar with the guilt the parents deal with of not being able to provide a happy home for their children and having to put them through the mental stress a divorce causes children. Sometimes, divorced parents tend to want to make up for a bad situation to their children by overcompensating — something that children pick up immediately. Whatever these kids ask for, the parents provide, sometimes when it is beyond their means to be able to provide.

> *A Yesaholic confesses:* "Last year my husband and I divorced. We have three small children, and I wanted to make the transition easier and less painful — that is when I became a Yesaholic. I would say Yes to everything the children wanted. They wanted a new game, I would say Yes and give in, thinking the game might take their mind off of the situation. The children wanted to have their friends over constantly for a sleepover, and I would say Yes, thinking it might be good for them. I continued to make concessions for the wrong reasons until the day when the requests became unbearable and too unreasonable, and then I realized I had made a mistake. Having made that realization, I decided it was time to bring this situation under control and started cutting back on the number of concessions I was making. I did not agree to buy every game or toy they wanted, and I did not allow them to have friends over to spend the night every time they asked. Little by little they learned that they could not always get a Yes answer to their wishes."

This parent had the best intentions in the world, but she said Yes too many times and for the wrong reason — guilt.

There are times when you say Yes out of guilt because you take into consideration how you felt when someone told you No under the same circumstances. However, realistically, the person you are telling No to may not necessarily feel or react the same way you did under those circumstances. Therefore, if you simply cannot commit, your answer should be No. People see and perceive things differently even under the same circumstances and react differently for various reasons. Just because your feelings were hurt the last time you invited your sister to your son's play and she could not make it does not mean she is going to feel the same way should you not be able to attend her daughter's ballet recital. Maybe she is not as sensitive or just does not let things bother her. If you absolutely cannot make it, then you cannot and should not let guilt guide you to doing otherwise.

You Should Have Your Needs Met

Every day that passes by is a moment in time that will never come back, which is why it is so important that you make time for yourself and see to it that your needs are met. Otherwise, you will live the rest of your life full of regrets about the things you wanted to do or could have done had you not been so busy tending to everybody else's needs. Look back on the last ten to 15 years of your life and reflect on how much you actually did for yourself. How much did you give up to take care of others? How much or how little were your needs met? Would you be happy with the decisions you made? Or, would you go back and change some of those decisions so that there was more time for you? The answer to this last question would probably be Yes because looking back, you are able to realize that in the process of being a great daughter or son, a great parent, a dedicated employee, and a great team member at whatever other activities you were involved in, your own needs were not met. You spent so much of your precious time volunteering at the PTA, taking care of family members, or going above and beyond your duties at work that you did not make time to go to the gym, take cake-decorating classes, or play baseball with the company team. So, the question is, are you willing to continue giving up your happiness for others? There is nothing wrong with helping others and being there for support when others need you; however, when you start depriving yourself of your needs and wants for those of others, you are being counterproductive. You may be trying to accomplish so much for the good of others, but are you really being able to give 100 percent of yourself toward the cause at hand when you may be feeling short-changed?

Life is so busy that if you keep on saying Yes to others, there will be not time for other productive things that will benefit you. It helps to be mindful of your desires and needs, so that when a request is made of you, it becomes easier to say No. A good suggestion may be for you to run through a self-check list before you answer Yes to any request — it will help make your decision a lot easier. Some questions you should ask yourself include the following:

1. *Do I really want to do this?*

You should never be forced to do something you do not want to do. Maybe the request goes against your beliefs, morals, or ethics. Sometimes it may just be because you do not really like the person who asked you and agreeing to such request would require you to spend time with them. Most important, if you know you are going to feel miserable carrying out whatever the task might have been, you certainly need to decline.

2. *Do I have time for this?*

Before responding to a request, evaluate if you actually have the time to spare to take care of whatever was asked of you. For example, if you already have a full schedule for Saturday between your kids' soccer games, grocery shopping, and a whole lot of other things you must accomplish, then why accept taking your friend's shift volunteering at the homeless shelter because she cannot go? The fact that she could not make her shift should not place the burden on you to take care of it for her because, realistically, you do not have the time. You will end up stressing and running around trying to accomplish things in the shortest amount of time so you can squeeze one more thing into your already filled day.

3. *Who, of the people I care the most about, will get shortchanged if I do this?*

Think about it — in the process of doing something for the world's good, you might end up taking time away from the people who mean the most to you. While devoting time you could be spending with your family to take care of someone else's needs, it is not uncommon to think your family will understand. You take for granted that because they love you, they will understand and will be OK with the situation. Your taking time away from them is not going to make them love you any less, but the time you do not spend with them is time that has been lost forever.

4. *Am I going to turn around and be mad at the person who asked because I said Yes to his/her request?*

Everybody has done it. Someone asks you to do something for him or her, you tell them "Yes, sure," but inside you are thinking, "This was a mistake. I should have never said Yes because I already have too much going on as it is." However, disregarding the voice in your head, you forge ahead only to get madder as you think more about the request to which you just agreed. So, what do you do? You get mad at the person who asked you for having asked you, instead of coming to terms with the fact that really you are just mad at yourself, and because you do not want to accept it, it is easier to get mad at the person who made the request. Then ask yourself, is it worth it? Is it worth getting mad at a relative, friend, or coworker because you could not get yourself to be strong enough to say No in the first place? The answer is, it is not worth it. It takes so much energy to be mad at someone, especially when they do not even know why you would be mad at them or that you are even mad at them. As far as they are concerned, there is no reason for anyone to be mad because they just asked for something to which you could have easily said No. In the end, you are on the losing end of the deal because not only are you now stuck doing something you do not want to do, but also you are spending precious energy that could be put to use on something productive, instead of being mad.

5. *Are there going to be irreparable consequences if I say No?*

In everyday life, the response to this question, more than likely, is going to be No. The situations people deal with on a daily basis with others making requests are just that — part of everyday requests that should still be appropriately evaluated before responding. However, if you are faced with a situation in which your answer would be "Yes, there will be irreparable consequences if I say No," then obviously your answer should be Yes.

6. Realistically, can someone else take care of this request other than me?

At times, someone may approach you to take care of something with such sense of urgency that your immediate reaction would be to say Yes immediately. However, giving it further thought, it might become apparent that you are not the only one in the world who can take care of such a task, that there are others who are as capable and probably willing to participate if they were to be asked. Think about the time you were asked to volunteer to sell tickets at your child's school for the school play coming up. When you were asked, you probably felt that you were being put on the spot and that you had to say Yes. Realistically, a number of other parents in the school could pick up that shift without any inconveniences, whereas you already had plans made for that afternoon that you would have to change to accommodate this request.

7. Does it fit within my priorities?

Putting things in perspective and prioritizing what is important to you makes your decision-making process a lot more painless and simpler. If something does not fit within your priorities, then do not do it

— it is that simple. Priorities mean just that — the things that are most important to you should be put above everything else. If someone asks something of you, and upon further evaluation, you realize that not only does it not fit within your priorities, but it is also something of little or no importance to you, then why agree? You have only so much time available to do the things you want to and need to do. Taking care of your priorities first is the only way you are going to be able to accomplish all that you have set out to do without overstressing yourself.

8. *How much time is going to be involved?*

How much time it will take you to accomplish a certain task is a critical factor as to whether you respond favorably to a request or whether you turn the request down. A call from your teenage daughter to pick up a display board for a project while you are already at the store will only add a minute or two to your trip to the store. However, a request from your mother to address her Christmas card envelopes is a different story. You know a task like this will be time-consuming, and you really should evaluate the request as to whether you have the time to do this for her without adding unnecessary stress to your life.

9. *Why am I really being asked?*

This is a good question to ask yourself when you have been asked to do something. Is the person doing the asking targeting you because he/she knows that you usually say Yes to all requests? Or, are you being asked because you really are the most qualified person to do it? If you know you are being asked because you usually say Yes, then at that moment you should put a stop to the vicious cycle and respond with a firm No. However, if you are being asked for any reason other than because you are a Yes person, then really evaluate the request, take in consideration the pros and cons of taking on the task, and make a decision that you will not regret later.

10. *Will I have this opportunity again at a more opportune time?*

There may be times when you are approached and asked to do something that you know you would enjoy doing, but you do not have the ability or the time take care of it. As you evaluate the request, you are torn between wanting to participate and knowing that, realistically, it would be impossible at that time. It is in those instances that you should take into consideration the probability that you will be able to take on this task later. For instance, someone approaches you and asks you if you would be willing to be the den mother of your son's Cub Scouts troop. It might be something you have thought about doing, but at this point in your life, it is impossible for you to take on this added responsibility. So, you decline the request, but you also state your desire to take on this task later when you have more free time to dedicate to it and do a good job.

Remember, there are only so many hours in a day to accomplish all that you have at hand. You can continue to add tasks to your day, but your day is not going to get any longer to accommodate your ever-growing list of things you want to or need to get done. As Steve Jobs, cofounder and chief executive officer of Apple, said in 2004 while being interviewed by the weekly business magazine *Bloomberg Businessweek*, "It comes from saying no to 1,000 things to make sure we don't get on the wrong track or try to do too much."

No is a Complete Sentence — There is no Need to Explain Further

Feeling the need to justify yourself when you say No is the biggest mistake you can make when you are trying to get out of doing something. When someone asks something of you, and you find yourself wanting to say No, then just say it. Although there are situations where just saying No may come across too harsh, there are other ways to convey a negative response without using the word No — as long as you keep it short, simple, and to the point. You do not need to go on with long explanations as to how "you would, but ...." Be decisive and use general statements such as:

"I am sorry, but I simply can't at this time." Some of the most difficult people to convince that your response is No are telemarketers. The reason being is that they are well trained to not only convince people to purchase their product or to donate to whatever worthy cause it is they are representing, but also they are trained to have a counter answer to each one of your No excuses. If the cause they are calling about is something you feel strongly about, and you wish to donate, then do so, but otherwise do not waste your time and energy dealing with people who will continue to nag on and on until they get what they want. There is no need for you to feel accosted in your own home by these annoying and oftentimes intruding calls. In those instances, simply tell them "I'm sorry, but I simply can't at this time," and proceed to hang up the telephone before they have an opportunity to come up with a response.

"I have a personal policy..." When responding No to someone, often you run the risk of the person taking your negative response personally, thereby creating an uncomfortable situation. By removing the personal connection between you, the request, and the person who made the request, you will be eliminating that problem. Your best bet is to reply that you have a personal policy

regarding that request. For instance, an employee asks you if he or she could borrow money from you until he or she gets paid the following week. As much as your initial reaction may be to lend the person some money because you know he or she needs it, by doing so you would be setting a precedence for other employees to come to you and ask for money. Telling some of your employees Yes and others No will definitely create a morale issue in your business. Therefore, your best option in such instances would be to tell the employee who is asking, "I understand your need, but I have a personal policy to never lend employees or friends money." That way the employee know it is not a personal denial and is instead what you would say to everyone.

"Let me think about it, and I'll get back with you." Or, *"It doesn't look like I'll be able to, but if anything changes, I'll let you know."* Using this response lets you buy time to think about the request and figure out whether you want to comply or decline. Especially when you are unsure about a request, it is easier to call the individual back and say that you cannot or will not be able to than replying Yes and then having to call back and say No. Creating a space of time between the request and the answer also has a tendency of softening up the decline of the request.

"It looks like I'm going to have to pass this time." When you tell someone that you are going to have to pass on their requests at this time, you are really telling them that

had the request been made at some other time, maybe you would have been able to comply. You are not making it look as if you have no interest in what they are asking of you, you are just letting them know that his is just not a good time for that. You are creating an easy exit for you out of the situation.

"I just can't fit it into my schedule." If you do not have any more room in your busy schedule for one more thing, then there is no use trying to squeeze something in when you know you will not be able to dedicate the appropriate time and effort the request may require. Or, it might be that you just absolutely do not have the time to spare to accommodate anything else. For instance, your friend calls in the morning and asks you to lunch that day. She tells you that she needs somebody to talk to because she is thinking about breaking up with her boyfriend and needs an opinion. The problem is that you have gone through this situation with her many times before — you have rearranged your schedule to fit her "emergency," and then it turns out it was just an emotional attack. You would love to be there for her as a friend, but you really have other very important things to take care of that day that cannot wait. Telling her that you just cannot fit her in is all that is necessary with no further explanation needed.

"That is such a good cause, but I am already supporting other good causes." There is no need to explain how many other causes or what the other causes may be. All you need

to let the person making the request know is that you are empathetic with the cause he or she is representing, but you will not be supporting his or her cause at this time.

"No, thank you." The word No in itself is clear, concise, and direct enough to make your point without needing further explanation. Adding "thank you" to the end of your No statement ends the statement in a much softer tone and communicates to the person making the request the unspoken statement that although you have to decline, you appreciate having been asked.

Just remember that if you start providing a lot of detail and all kinds of reasons as to why you cannot, the other person will try to find a solution for each one of your excuses. Be firm and most of all, honest. Do not make up a story that you are going to have a hard time backing up later on because in trying to get out of something you may create for yourself a bigger problem — being taken as a dishonest person. Honesty and sincerity will take you a long way. When you tell someone No to a request, and the reason you give him or her is an honest one, they will remember that and more than likely, be understanding of your No. However, should you tell someone No and make up this convoluted story to make yourself look good, the person could find out it was a dishonest excuse, and they will never feel the same way about you. It could jeopardize friendships, relationships, and even business relations.

Also simple, but effective, is adding "thanks" or "thank you" at the end of your No statement. It has a magical way of softening your negative response. Adding "thanks" or "thank you" does not allow the person to whom you just said No to get upset. How can they? You said No, but were so polite about it that it would be difficult for them to get upset at you.

It is important for your needs to be met and your feelings and wants to be taken into consideration when saying No. However, as much as you may consider all this when making a decision as to whether you should say Yes or No, other factors come into play. Some of these factors, such as cultural imprinting and your upbringing, subconsciously cloud your reasoning and keep you from making a decision that best meets your needs.

you say yes because you were brought up that way

THE BRITISH ANTHROPOLOGIST SIR EDWARD Burnette Tylor defined culture as "that complex whole which includes knowledge, belief, art, morals, law, custom, and any other capabilities and habits acquired by man as a member of society." Culture embodies learned patterns of behavior — ways of feeling, acting, and thinking — rather than patterns determined biologically. Therefore, it is fair to say that people are products of their cultural conditioning. However, regardless of what culture you originate from, there are some commonalities just as there are distinct differences among them. For instance, being polite and respecting authority is common among many cultures, both of which are deep-rooted causes for people to continuously say Yes when they should be saying No.

In addition to the conditioning with which people were brought up, the old cultural barriers, although they are not as intense as they use to be, are, nevertheless, very present in their everyday lives. Fortunately, for generations people have been striving to make positive changes in our society to improve everyone's quality of life. Some of these changes are made due to changes in laws and regulations that force people to accept new ways of doing things. Other changes take place individually, such as it would be the case with people taking a stand and saying No, making a statement for what they believe in individually.

People of All Walks of Life Have Trouble Saying No

It is not just in the American culture that you find people with the inability to say No when they normally say Yes. It would be safe to say that this behavior is just people's overall desire to help and please others. In the American culture, it is possible that this behavior stems from the more subservient culture that was brought to America by the early settlers. When discussing the issue of usually saying Yes when you should say No with people from other cultures, you should recognize that in some cultures this is more of a prevalent situation than in others. For instance, people from East Asia avoid saying No to each other's requests as much as possible, especially when the request is being made within a close relationship such as family. In Latin countries where there is still more of a subservient environment between men and women, there is more of a tendency for women to say Yes more often than

No. Regardless of the culture, saying Yes out of respect and politeness seems to be a common thread among people.

Another aspect to take into consideration while trying to break the cycle of continuously saying Yes is the fact that women more frequently feel the need to explain why they cannot comply with a request than men do. When men are in a situation where they need to respond Yes or No, if their response is going to be No, most of the time they just say No and offer little or no explanation. Depending on the circumstances, there is normally no guilt attached to their No, and they will give little to no thought to the situation afterward. Women, on the other hand, generally are more compelled to offer a detailed explanation as why they cannot respond positively to a request. Not only do women feel the need to explain, they also are more likely to continue to think about the issue afterward and build a sense of guilt because even though they managed to muster the courage to say No, women will still wonder later if they should have said Yes. For instance, examine the same scenario where in one instance the protagonist is a man and in the other one the protagonist is a woman. The outcome of these scenarios is totally different.

One of Tom's friends from high school, Alex, is getting married. Although it has been four years since they have seen each other, they have remained in touch, communicating online occasionally. Recently, Alex contacts Tom as asks him to be one the groomsmen in his wedding party. He further explains that his wife-to-be had selected six bridesmaids and, therefore, he has to come up with six groomsmen. Alex explains to Tom that he remembered what good friends they had been in school and thought maybe he wanted to be part of his wedding. He further explains that the wedding's budget is tight so Alex needs Tom to pay all his expenses, such as tuxedo rental and travel expenses. Tom gives the request some brief consideration and realizes that Alex is not that special of a friend to warrant him taking vacation time from work and incurring all the expenses to attend Alex's wedding. Tom tells Alex that he appreciates him thinking of him, but he is not going to be able to be part of the wedding. Tom offers no further explanation and as far as he is concerned, the issue is over.

One of Katie's friends from high school, Anna, is getting married. Although it has been four years since they had seen each other, they have remained in touch, communicating online once in a while. Recently Anna contacts Katie and asks her to be one of the bridesmaids in her wedding party. Anna further explains that her fiancé has six friends whom he wants to be his groomsmen and, therefore, she now has to find six bridesmaids for the wedding. Anna continues on to explain to Katie how she remembered what good friends they had been in school and thought that maybe she wanted to be part of her wedding. She further explains that they have to pay for the wedding themselves and are trying to cut corners and save money wherever possible, so she (Anna) needs Katie to pay for all her own expenses. She would need Katie to pay for the bridesmaid dress, as well as travel and lodging expenses to attend the wedding. After Katie tells Anna how excited and happy she is for her, Katie asks Anna for the details of the wedding and tells her without much hesitation that she would love to be there for her on that very special day. When the conversation is over, Katie realizes that she should have told Anna No because they are not that good of friends anymore. Anna did not invite her as an initial thought. It was an afterthought out of necessity of gathering a total of six bridesmaids, and it was going to cost her a small fortune to attend this wedding. At that point, Katie could have kicked herself for not having had the courage to have said No, even if she had told Anna to let her think about it to later reply that she could not accept the invitation.

Scenarios look familiar? Probably yes, because people are accustomed to that kind of behavior and have come to expect it in their culture.

Breaking through old cultural barriers

Although people today still display patterns of behavior based on traditional cultural values, people seem to be more assertive and sure of themselves than in previous generations. People take more chances and are more likely to take on new ventures, all of which involve having said many Yeses along the way. However, multiple cultural barriers still must be broken through to enable people to be more assertive and take their appropriate place, saying No when necessary.

Great strides have been made in society because of people standing up and saying No to unacceptable or unfair situations. For instance, one of the biggest movements asserting equality for men and women, thereby saying No to men having certain rights over women, was the movement that led to women winning the right to vote in 1920. By remaining quiet, women were saying Yes to the conviction that men were superior to women and deserving of the right to vote. When women finally stood up and took action in the matter, their voices were heard loud and clear. Saying No to an unjust situation had a ripple effect that still affects our nation today.

Cultural diversity in the workplace continues to rise as people from all cultural and ethnic backgrounds come together to work toward a common goal. However, with such increase in diversity came the inevitable issue of misunderstandings with people anticipating what traits a person will bring to the job because of his or her ethnic background. Unfortunately, at times, people assume that some cultures or ethnic groups are more submissive and less assertive than others, thereby generating an uneven playing field. An interesting report that addresses this issue was published in the *Management Development Forum,* which is sponsored by the Empire State College in New York. The *Management Development Forum* is a journal specializing in management and organizational development that collects and disseminates information on new theories and knowledge in the management field. The report, titled "Cultural Impact of Non-Assertiveness of East Asian Subordinates," was the result of a study conducted by Jensen Chung in which he was trying to determine if individuals of East Asian descent were in fact lacking leadership abilities or were just being perceived as not assertive individuals.

The study revealed that Asian-American engineers felt as if superiors or even coworkers were taking advantage of what was perceived to be a weakness, and these engineers were skipped for promotions, as well as given a heavier workload. One of the elements of the study involved conducting interviews of Asian-American engineers in high-tech industries, which revealed that their nonconfrontational cultural imprint made it seem as if they were lacking leadership skills. Those interviewed further revealed how, due to their deep-rooted cultural imprinting, they were less likely to say No to requests made by their superiors, even when it was beyond the scope of their work.

Fortunately, times have changed, and as the gap between minorities and non-minorities continues to close, the atmosphere in today's society is such that all individuals are equal with the same rights to say No. Old mindsets are being dissipated, and the old cultural barriers that made it more difficult for people to feel comfortable saying No are virtually nonexistent.

There is More Room for No's In Today's World Than Ever Before

The way people function in society today is quite different from years ago. Mindsets toward people based on their sex, race, religion, and such differ from opinions in the past. For instance, in the past, women were expected to be submissive and obedient to their husbands. They were not equals, and, as such, women were expected to always comply with their husbands' requests regardless of how differently the wife might have felt about it. Replying with a No to a husband's request several decades ago was completely unheard of. Little by little, women have made a place for themselves in society where saying No is acceptable and even expected at times. Women have learned that they can still be great mothers, wives, employees, and members of the community without having to say Yes to everyone's requests. Women, increasingly, are being encouraged to start saying No to taking on so many tasks because it has been proven that taking on too much is not mentally or physically healthy.

In the past, children did not have any rights. They had absolutely no right to say No even if it was to stop abusive behavior, regardless of the behavior's severity. Today, children are taught to be aware of unsafe situations and are more empowered to stand up and say No when necessary. Society is teaching children to be more confident and strong and say No to drugs, drinking, and even bullying. Skills that children are learning today will be valuable to them in the future as they continue to grow and become valuable members of society. It also provides them with the groundwork necessary to enable them to learn to say No as they face different circumstances throughout their lives that will keep them from taking on more than they can handle.

The same inability to speak up and say No when desired was true for individuals who were of lower social status in the society. Poor, uneducated people were expected always to comply with the requests of those of higher social status. People of the lower class were expected to be obedient and unquestioning of the requests made by those of a higher class. Poor people were often treated unfairly and unjustly, sometimes to extremes without the ability to stand up and say No. Fortunately, that is not the case anymore. Regardless of class or social status, everyone has the right to say No without the fear of repercussion from anyone.

As a whole, society has come a long way in treating everyone fairly and allowing everybody to have a voice that needs to be heard. It is your job now to exercise that ability and learn to say No when that is what you really want to and need to say. Although society as a whole has become more accepting of people saying No when normally they would have been expected to say Yes, you need to make that change within yourself and try to leave behind old behaviors so that you can be assertive and say No. With a little bit of effort, you will be successful at not giving much weight to what people may think or whether it is that important to belong to a certain group that will warrant your saying Yes when you really want to say No.

CHAPTER FOUR

but nobody will like me if i say no

EVERYONE WANTS TO BE LIKED, AND, AT TIMES, SOME people go over the limits to do whatever it takes to get people to like them. However, the reality is there are always going to be people out there who do not like you. Plenty of people will like you, but not everyone. When you really think about it, you do not like everyone you know either. So, putting it into that perspective may help you realize that it is OK not to be liked by everyone because you do not like everyone you know. Therefore, saying Yes to people's requests so that they will continue to like you or make them like you is futile. You will be wasting energy and precious time on something that, in the overall scheme of things, is just not that important. The important thing is that you like yourself, and you should consider yourself first before you try to please everybody in an effort to be liked.

Fear of Rejection

Fear of rejection can stem from lack of self-esteem. People seem to put too much value into what people think or how they may feel about them, thereby constantly trying to meet some self-imposed standard they feel must meet in order for others to like them. The fear of rejection will certainly drive you to say Yes every time you are asked to do something so you can prove how wonderful you are and avoid being rejected in the future by the person who asked.

A Yesaholic confesses: "Last week, after months of being divorced, I started dating Stacy. She seemed like a nice girl. We had a lot of things in common and really enjoyed each other's company. The only problem is that Stacy's religious beliefs and practices are very different from mine and my close group of friends. This group of friends in particular is a support group from my church that has been by my side during the worst of times. My friends did not want to accept Stacy into the group, insisting that Stacy's influence would drive me away from the church. It got to the point where I could no longer attend support group meetings or social activities with them without being pushed in some way to break the relationship with Stacy. They kept insisting that I should try to find someone who shared our same beliefs. Feeling a little left out by my friends and as if I was losing my support group, I gave in and broke up with Stacy. Although I did not date Stacy very

> long, by saying Yes to my friends, I cheated myself out
> of an opportunity to foster a relationship with someone
> who was a little different from me. Now I regret it
> because I could have learned a great deal from her,
> and she could have learned a lot from me as well."

Sometimes for fear of being rejected, you give up things that are important to you, such as relationships, as well as time you could be doing something you enjoy. Not wanting to be judged and rejected, sometimes you agree to go do things with your friends that may not be exactly what you want to do, but you feel like at least your group of friends is not rejecting you. Instead, you should speak up and say what you really want to do, regardless of how you may be judged or even rejected. You can join other groups of friends who share your interests.

As Mahatma Gandhi said, "A No uttered from deepest conviction is better and greater than a Yes merely uttered to please, or what is worse, to avoid trouble."

Doing whatever it takes, even saying Yes, to belong

Belonging is one of the top three basic human needs, just above health and safety, according to Maslow's hierarchy of needs. Abraham Maslow is one of the originators of a humanist approach to management. In 1943, Maslow wrote an unprecedented paper that listed the five fundamental human needs, starting from bottom up, with the most fundamental need at the base of the hierarchical pyramid. From bottom to top, the needs are listed as physiological, safety, belonging, esteem, and self-actualization. Further, according to Maslow's hierarchy of needs, even though the need to belong includes love and affection, often people will prefer not to be loved as much by a group they belong to, rather than not belonging to a group at all.

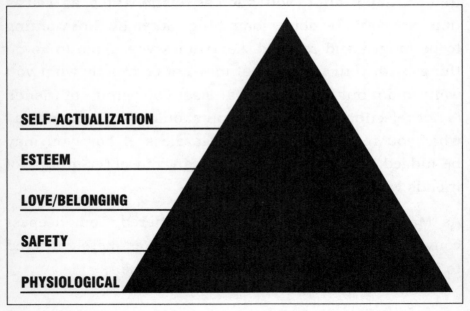

SELF-ACTUALIZATION

ESTEEM

LOVE/BELONGING

SAFETY

PHYSIOLOGICAL

Regardless of how much any culture values independence, people are still bound by a strong sense of belonging. Needing to feel a sense of belonging is why many people will give in to peer pressure — usually by following and adapting to certain expectations whether they truly believe in those expectations or not — just to belong to a group. Peer pressure is one of today's culture's worst problems, not only because it preys on people's need to belong, but also because it strips them from maintaining their individuality. When you agree to something, especially when it is out of a need to belong, you are giving up your individuality because you are no longer acting out of your own individual needs and desires, but rather out of what the others need or want.

Giving in to peer pressure because you want to belong and be accepted by others is the wrong path to follow. At times, saying Yes and giving in to peer pressure can have disastrous results. Although everyone is subjected to peer pressure during different times throughout their lives, adults seem not to give in as easily as the younger crowd. For children, teenagers, and young adults, it is not as easy to stand up for what they believe in, oftentimes, they readily give in so that they can belong. Teaching children and young adults to foster their sense of individuality rather than giving in to peer pressure may be an uphill battle, but it is a worthwhile battle to fight. The number of incidents of underage drinking and smoking is staggering. These young adults are saying Yes to peer pressure, subjecting themselves to unhealthy situations, just to belong. It is important to realize that although getting rid of that deep-rooted need to belong is nearly impossible, managing that need wisely can have positive outcomes rather than negative ones.

Learning to say No to such destructive activities is one of the most valuable lessons anyone can ever learn. The less complicated the No answer is, the easier it is to say. Keeping the responses simple and honest will give your statement that much more validity.

Express Your Decision with Conviction

An old saying goes that nothing has been ever written about cowards, but heroes have many books. Not being afraid to step up to the plate and say "No, I can't," is a lot more honorable than saying Yes while thinking of all the reasons why you should have said No. When you speak with assertiveness and authority, people will pick upon that and respond accordingly. If you respond No with confidence, and you are sure of what you are saying, there is not much room for the person who is asking to work a Yes out of you.

However, when you are uncertain, people also pick up on this and take advantage of it immediately, which is when they start telling you all the reasons why you should say Yes instead of No. They find a solution to every one of your weak excuses until the point where you are backed into a corner where there is no way out other than just saying Yes. Delivering a firm and clear No does not leave room for negotiating a different answer.

Sometimes delivering a definitive No answer does not come easily. It is like any other skill; it must be learned and practiced in order for it to come out naturally and be effective. Here are some steps you can take that will help you come up with a very assertive No.

1. **Take a moment before you answer:** Taking a moment to think about the request and assess the situation, rather than uttering your response without thinking, will add validity to your response. The individual who is asking will realize that you are actually giving his or her request some consideration, which means you consider such a request important. Taking this step alone will soften the effects when you respond No because the person will feel that you actually gave it some serious consideration.

2. **Buy yourself some time:** Not all requests require a Yes or No answer on the spot. If you can buy yourself some time, go ahead and do it. Say something like "Let me check my schedule, and I'll get back to you." Another good one to use is, "I believe we already have plans, but I'll double check and get back with you." Take advantage of the gap in time to evaluate the request and decide what you really want to do. Practice how you will say No or to come up with a solid, concrete response that will command respect and authority, thereby eliminating the possibility of the asking party trying to negotiate.

3. **Make a decision and stick to it:** Once you make a decision to say No, stick to it. That is why you should really evaluate the request while you are buying yourself some time. If you say No and then

call back the person making the request and say "You know, actually I can...." you might have just opened yourself up for nagging in future situations. The person making the request now knows that although you initially say No, there is a possibility that you will change your mind. Next time they ask you for something, and you say No, you can count on them coming back to you again, hoping for a change of heart.

4. **Give them an answer — just say No:** Here is where you make your statement firm and convincing and without a lot of fluff. End the subject, and move on to another conversation before giving the person making the request an opportunity to even think about negotiating or making you feel guilty.

In the end, building a reputation for yourself as a person who sticks to his or her word and is sure of him or herself will prevent people from trying to take advantage of you in the future. They will accept your No answers and will respect you and your decisions. This includes your friends and family who are so accustomed to your usually saying Yes and expecting you to comply with their requests because you are a friend. There is nothing wrong with being assertive enough to say No occasionally to friends and still feel confident that the friendship will remain.

saying no to friends

FRIENDS PLAY A VERY IMPORTANT ROLE IN YOUR LIFE, especially your best friends. Acquaintances can be many, but friends only a few. You know who your acquaintances are because you only see them from time to time. You cannot really count on them to be there for you in the good, the bad, and the ugly. They normally are mostly around for the good. These individuals, however, have a way of remembering you and knowing just where to find you when they need something. So, if there ever is a toss-up between doing something for a friend or doing something for an acquaintance, there should be no doubt that doing something for the friend wins.

How Do You Say No to a True Friend?

True friends are there for you when you need them, and you are there for them in times of need as well. Friends sometimes play even a bigger role in your life than your own family. As people move away from their hometowns, they might lose the support they once had from having their family close by and start to develop closer relationships with friends, taking the role of family to each other. That is not to say that you completely sever your ties with your family because you are not physically close any more, but it is not the same as having somebody there to care for you should you be sick or want to spend some quality time together. During difficult times, for instance, it makes a great difference to have friends to lean on and cry on their shoulders, rather than an e-mail from your sister who lives across the country to tell you it is going to be OK.

That is why it is so difficult to say No to friends whenever they ask something of you. Regardless of how significant or insignificant their request may be or how capable or incapable you may be of complying with their request, there is always the guilt factor. You cannot help but feel compelled to agree to comply with each one of their requests because they are your friends, and you know they are counting on you. But you must realize that because they are your friends, they should understand that you are not always able to say Yes. Remember, there are times when you have asked something of them, and they have not been able to help you. Were you understanding of their decline? More than likely, you were. Because of the friendship that exists between you and your friends, you are certain that that if they could have been there for you, they would have.

When you have to tell a friend No to a certain request, remind him or her just how important he or she is to you and how much he or she means to you, but you just have to say No at this time. Depending on your relationship with your friend, sometimes a simple, "I'm sorry but I can't help you with that right now," will suffice. There are other times, however, when the friend is one of those who is full of self-pity and in need of constant reassurance, and those No's need to be a little more empathetic to meet your friend's needs. The last thing you want is to lose a friendship over an unnecessarily harsh No. You know your friends better than anyone else, and in any long-term friendship there will always be plenty of situations when you will have to tell each other No. However, in a long and happy friendship, it is important to know each individual's needs and expressing those No's accordingly.

CASE STUDY: WESLEY BAKER

Full-time Student and student office assistant at the University of Florida Gainesville, Florida

CLASSIFIED CASE STUDIES
directly from the experts

As a full-time student and part-time employee at the University of Florida, Wesley Baker keeps a very busy schedule. In addition to school and work responsibilities, his desire to stay in touch with his family and friends also takes a great deal of his time. Being a people person, he wants to be everywhere for everybody, saying Yes more often than he probably should. His pattern of saying Yes to people at work, his friends, and family often leads to conflicts of interest with things that he should be doing.

The problem, according to Baker, is that although, on occasion, he takes time to consider the request before answering, he still says Yes and ends up stretching himself too thin. So, he ends up saying Yes to too many people, thereby leaving little time for himself. Consequently, he often regrets having said Yes rather than just having said No. After saying Yes to someone when he knew he should have said No, he is usually faced with the dilemma of either getting back in touch with the person and having to change his answer or just accept his decision and do what he said he would.

He realizes that saying Yes to too many people means that he is trying to cram too many people/events/things into too small a time frame and ends up stressed out, upset, and often is unable to enjoy the events to the fullest because he is constantly checking his watch to see when he has to be on his way to the next event. However, regardless of his efforts to please everyone, he still upsets people at times because he often does not stay in any one event from beginning to end, as he has to be on his way somewhere else. So, when he knows he has upset people because he has either left before the event was over or arrived late, he gets upset at himself because it was never his intention to hurt anyone's feelings.

Baker feels that the main reason why he says Yes more often than he should is because he feels that he is a people person, and he wants people to feel that they can come to him when they need something and he will be there for them. He said, "I truly stick by my friends and family, and if they ever need anything, even if it means missing out on something I wanted to do. I have always been driven to help people and be there for people when they need me." He admits that his desire to help people has made it very difficult for him to be able to say No so far.

How Can You Prevent Your Feelings From Getting in the Way of Saying No?

Sometimes friends will make unrealistic requests assuming you will agree to the request because of the friendship. Do not let your feelings get in the way of saying No. Think with your head and not your heart, and you may just avoid an unpleasant situation for both of you. When such unrealistic requests are made, you may diffuse the situation by making your friends realize just how unfair they are being by making such requests of you. Sometimes the best way to make your friends realize how unfair they are being is to ask your friends if they would be willing to do the same for you if you asked them for help with such unrealistic requests. Insist that they answer you honestly.

For instance, one of your best friends from high school, Anya, who now lives in New York, wants to come visit you in Florida in a couple of weeks. You would not have a problem with her coming and staying at your home with you and your family, but the problem is that Anya wants to come visit with her new boyfriend of only a couple of months. You know Anya well, however, you do not know Anya's boyfriend at all. You tell Anya that you would love to have her if she was coming alone, however, not having yet met her boyfriend, you do not feel comfortable having a stranger spend the night at your house. As she tries to convince you to accept, you then ask her if she would do the same for you under the same circumstances, thereby putting things into perspective. The chances are that, being the true friend she is, she will realize the uncomfortable situation that she is putting you in and desist from her request.

Are They Really Your Friends, or Are They Just Using You?

On the other hand, there are people who pretend to be your friends but in reality are just using you. For some reason, it seems that everyone needs at least one of those in their lives. These are the people who are around you for convenience, and although they may not be in touch constantly, they remain in touch often enough to make it seem like they really care. They constantly need something from you, but because they are staying in touch on a regular basis, their calls for requests are just intermingled with other calls so it is not so obvious they are really calling because they need something. These are people who call you on Monday and ask how your weekend went, make small talk, and then end the conversation. Then, they call you again on Thursday and ask you if they can borrow your boat over the weekend if you are not going to be using it. The following week, they may call for a few minutes to tell you they were thinking about you and wondering how you were doing, but that is only because a few days later they are calling to see if they can come over on Saturday to let their kids swim in your pool.

These are just a couple of examples of totally unacceptable behavior people experience from supposed friends. They do not call you and invite you over for a cookout on the weekend or offer to come help you with your next small project on the house. They are obviously in the "friendship" for their benefit only. There is no give and take in this situation. It is all about them and what they can get out of this relationship. Unfortunately, a lot of people have had similar experiences, and sometimes, it takes a while to realize that they are taking advantage of you. Nevertheless, once you make that realization, it is time for some assertive and straightforward No's. When they ask, "Can I borrow your RV this weekend to take my in-laws to the beach?" your response should be, "No, you can't." When they tell you that they might as well stay over for dinner when they come to pick up the kids after a ball game, you tell them, "No, you may not. We have other plans."

There are also those "friends" who like to use you for their own self-esteem trip. They are supposed to be your friends, but they use you every chance they get to make themselves look better in front of others. For instance, one friend might openly talk about how you know each other from college and how you stayed friends through college even though you were not able to make it into a fraternity like he did. Obviously, he is putting himself at a completely different, and higher, social status than you while you were both in college. HIs underlying theme: he was way cooler and more popular than you because a group did not accept you but accepted him. In other words, he might be your friend, but you are not "as good" as he is. Others might make constant comments about your height, or lack thereof. They are the first ones to push you to the front in group pictures or make comments about how short people cannot afford to gain a lot of weight, or it shows. They are supposedly making all these comments not meaning anything by it. Or better yet, they say they can make these comments because they are your "friends," and you should know they do not mean anything by it.

The truth is that you know they do mean what they are saying, but they are just cowards hiding behind the veil of "friendship" to make themselves look better at your expense. The solution to this situation and the way to put an end to it is saying No to all of it. Do not allow them to continue; insetad speak up. Not saying anything in response to actions such as the ones mentioned here is practically saying Yes to such behavior and agreeing to it. Regardless of how much you disapprove and despise such behavior, your nonverbal response allows them to continue such behavior, belittling and humiliating you along the way. You can say No to such actions by making statements such as:

- "I thought you were my friend, and friends don't treat friends that way."

- "I am tired of your demeaning comments, you need to stop."

- "Your comments about my height are really starting to hurt my feelings."

- "I know you think it was funny, but I don't appreciate being made fun of."

- "Having friends like you, I don't need any enemies."

When dealing with people like this, not only do you have to learn how to say No to their requests, but you need to really get them out of your life. Having faux friends such as the ones mentioned in these examples will only drain you, both physically and mentally. You get so frustrated with them that you spend precious energy being mad at them and thinking of ways to get rid of them, aside from all the time and effort you might have already invested in taking care of some of their requests.

Saying No to your disconcerting friends

Several types of friends fall in the category of a disconcerting friend. There are the friends who only call when they need something, the ones that talk about nothing other than themselves, and the ones who overtake conversations to talk about all the things they have done and know about, whether they are true or not. These people for the most part tend to be rude, self-centered, and inconsiderate. Although you really cannot change who they are, the fact that you share some kind of friendship with them means that somewhere along the line, you found traits or characteristics in these people that were appealing to you. It is a widely known fact that no one is perfect, but sometimes people like these can truly drive you up a wall.

The friends who only call you when they need something certainly can make you angry because it is inconsiderate. You might have known them for years, and although there may not be constant or regular communication between both of you, you know the connection exists, and you still consider them your friends/acquaintances. The only difference between you and these friends/acquaintances is that they only call when they need something from you, unlike you, who might call from time to time just to see how they are doing. For instance, they did not call you or go visit you at the hospital when you had a car accident and were hospitalized for a week. For that matter, they made themselves quite scarce when you lost your job and were not having parties at your house anymore. What is worst, they did not even pick up the telephone to call you and spend a few minutes telling you how sorry they were when your father died. However, they do not bat an eye before calling you to ask if you can take them to the airport so they do not have to pay for parking while on vacation. They will call you to invite themselves over to spend the weekend with you at your beach condo, even if you have never invited them before.

Putting an end to this type of behavior is not easy, and it takes some effort. Just as they are extremely disconnected with the fact they are being rude and not being good friends, they do not get it when you politely try to say No to them. They just do not seem to understand why you get upset at their uninvited intrusions and their lack of communication other than when they need something. Being the person who usually says Yes, you are going to be very conscious of how you say No to these people without hurting their feelings. But the truth is that they obviously have no concern for your feelings, or they would not be behaving this way. Therefore, a firm "No, you cannot come over for the weekend," or "No, I cannot take you to the airport" should be sufficient without having to offer further explanation. After saying No enough times to these individuals, maybe they will get the point.

How about those friends who have the uncanny habit of talking about nothing but themselves? They love to talk about their lives, their accomplishments, their kids' accomplishments, and even their dogs, but it never occurs to them to even ask how you have been. They monopolize conversations by talking about all they have done, places they have been, and all the things they know. It does not take many of these self-centered conversations to turn you completely off and make you feel like you just want to run away. The question is: Why do you let them get away with it and let them continue to ramble on about themselves without putting a stop to it? Probably because you consider them friends, and you know that telling them they are being self-centered when they only talk about themselves will not go over well. In addition, aside from this critical downfall, you like them as people, so you try to overcome their flaws and continue to spend time with them. Therefore, if you really care about the relationship, before reaching that point of not being able to take it anymore, you should let them know how you feel and that you would enjoy the conversations with them even more if you were to talk about other things, such as what is going on in your life or with your children. By allowing them to control the conversations constantly discussing the wonderfulness of being them, you are silently saying Yes to them, thereby approving this conduct.

A Yesaholic confesses: "My friend Linda and I have been friends for what seems like forever. She is a good friend in that she is always there for me when I need her, and we seem to enjoy the same things. The only problem is that Linda has the bad habit of wanting to be the center of attention whenever we are at a social setting by talking about all the things she has done in her lifetime and all the places she has been. As if that were not bad enough, she wants to outdo whatever anyone else says in the conversation even if it entails making it up. It makes me crazy when she does that, and I get totally embarrassed because I cannot help but wonder what other people there are thinking. Do they think I have made up stories as well because we are close friends? They obviously can tell she is making the stories up as she goes along, and I want to tell her so badly to stop. I just don't know how to bring an end to this disturbing behavior other than just telling her how I feel, emphasizing that it is for her own good. I would risk having her upset at me for a while, but I am sure she will get over it, and it will certainly be worth it."

As difficult as this situation may be, being assertive with your friend and letting him or her know how much you disapprove of this behavior is the only way you will ever be able to save this friendship from collapsing due to your getting tired of putting up with him or her railroading conversations and lying his or her way through it. Again, as in the situations discussed previously, unless you verbally express your displeasure and ask your friend to discontinue such activities, there is an unspoken Yes that says, "Go ahead, I am fine with your actions."

Will My Friends Get Their Feelings Hurt if I Say No?

You know you have a true friend when they worry more about saving and fostering a relationship than resenting your having said No to a request they made. Between friends, requests for help and support are constantly mutually made. However, creating a sense of trust that extends to the point of not resenting and accepting when a friend cannot do something for you is essential to maintaining any healthy relationship.

Agonizing over considering saying No to a friend should not even be an option. Normally, good friends know you well enough to know that when you say No to a plea for something, it is because you absolutely cannot comply. They will understand and move on. Some may ask for an explanation, probably out of concern, while others may not even feel the need to ask why you were not able to accept. A true friend not only will ask out of concern, but also if the reason that you cannot accept is because you have too much on your plate. They may even try to help instead of wasting time trying to convince you otherwise. It is much better for you to be honest with your friends and tell them No to a request when you cannot comply, rather than trying to squeeze whatever it is in your schedule and then not have your heart in it.

Between true friends, there is an unspoken understanding that in times of need you will do everything possible to be there for each other, whatever the case may be. There is also the understanding that there may be times when regardless of how badly you want to be there for them, you are just not able.

For instance, your best friend Chris calls you and tells you that in a couple of weeks he will be moving from his current apartment to a different apartment across town. He asks if you could come help him move. Aside from actually needing help moving the furniture, he also needs help taking some furniture apart the night before the actual move as he is trying to pay for the moving truck for only one day. You tell him you have to check your calendar and get back to him to make sure you are available that weekend. As it turns out, your son has a soccer tournament that weekend, and you have been helping as an assistant coach, so you really cannot skip the tournament. Not only is it imperative that you are there as assistant coach, but you also need to be there to support your son's game. You call Chris and explain the situation, letting him know how much you would like to help, but just are not able to do it that weekend. Being a good friend, Chris understands your No and asks if it would be better if he were to change the move for the weekend before or the weekend after. As either weekend works out fine with you, arrangements are made, and you are then able to both attend your son's soccer tournament and help your friend move.

When there is a mutual understanding, both parties win, and there are no hard feelings resulting from your inability to comply with a certain request.

Will My Friends Understand Why I Said No?

There are instances when saying No to friends is more out of concern for their well-being, and, at times, your own, than for any other reason. There also are times when, although it may not seem like it at the moment, it is best to say No to friends because, in the end, it will be healthier for your relationship than complying with the request and possibly ruining a great friendship. In circumstances when your friend asks you to do something illegal for him or her or cover up for them, it is in everyone's best interest that you decline rather than accept because it is a friend making the request.

Your underage friend asking you to purchase alcohol or cigarettes for them is an example of those instances when it is in your friend's best interest that you say No. Not only is it illegal for him or her to consume the alcohol or smoke the cigarettes, it is illegal for you to purchase it for him or her. Therefore, when you put things into perspective, it is easy to realize that it is not worth the risk of facing the legal ramifications this action will have over having a friend be upset at you for a while. If they really are your friends, they eventually will realize you did it for their own good as well as your own and get over it.

Another common scenario is when friends ask you to cover for them. At work, either they are calling in sick to go watch the ball game and ask you to back them up when they say they are sick, or when they make a major mistake and ask you to help them cover it up so the boss will not fire them. No one wants to face these situations. You are torn between being a faithful and loyal friend covering up for them, thereby being prepared to deal with the ramifications of being involved, or saying No and taking the honest route. Although you would like to think that a good friend would not put you in such situations, it happens more often than you probably care to know. Here is where your being a truly good friend is put to the test. The morally and ethically correct response to either one of these requests should be No and a decline to participate in your friend's dishonest actions. The consequences of wanting to help a friend at all costs, regardless of the situation, can be devastating for you. Just imagine what the boss's reaction will be once he or she finds out you were aware of such dishonest behavior and willingly participated by covering for your friend. More than likely, your boss's opinion about your honesty and work ethics will never be the same, probably affecting the future of your career at that workplace or hindering your chances for promotion in the future.

There are times when loaning money to a friend can ruin a friendship. When someone is in a financial bind, whether they are short $50 or $1,000, he or she tends to turn to a friend for assistance. The problem is that, as a friend, you want to help him or her because you certainly do not want to see your friend going through that kind of situation. However, regardless of the fact that you have the money available to lend, you must really give such requests a lot of consideration before you agree or disagree to help your friend. Is this particular friend good with his or her word about paying money back? Or, is this the kind of friend who takes advantage of the friendship to not pay you back or takes forever to pay you back?

Loaning money to a friend is a very tricky situation. If you do not lend the money, more than likely, there will be some very hard feelings from your friend, especially if he or she knows you are financially capable of loaning that money. It will be hard for him or her to understand that your friendship is worth more than any amount of money you could lend, but you are trying to avoid a situation where the friendship goes bad because of the loan. On the other hand, if you do loan the money, you are running the risk of him or her not paying you back or taking his or her time paying you back, which also creates a lot of bad feelings between friends. In either case, the chances are good that one of the two parties involved will end up feeling let down by the other friend, often ending the relationship. If you are the one lending the money and do not get paid back, you will have hard feelings toward your friend. If you are the friend asking for the money, and you get turned down, you will then be the one with the hard feelings toward your friend for not having loaned you the money.

So the question remains, it is worth it to risk so much because you could not muster the courage to tell your friends No? I am sure you will agree, the answer is No.

It is not easy telling your friends No when they ask something of you because there is that unspoken understanding that "that's what friends are for," and you feel like you should be there for each other. Although that is true, you should always be there for each other within reason, trying to keep in mind that, at times, there are limitations as to just how much you can do for others. Because in the process of always being there for your friend, you may end up not being there for yourself — keeping you from taking care of your needs by putting their needs first. This is even a more common occurrence when it comes to family because there seems to be an even stronger sense of duty and responsibility that has been deeply ingrained since childhood.

saying no to family

SAYING NO TO FAMILY MEMBERS IS PROBABLY MORE difficult than saying No to acquaintances, business relations, or even friends. With family members, there are certain expectations because of the family bond, and you feel more of an obligation to cater to your family. Not only do you feel that there is an obligation to comply, but your family also feels that there is somewhat of an obligation for you to comply — as if it was expected. Breaking away from this pattern of behavior is not easy. You are so "programmed" to respond to each request that your family members make that you respond without giving it much thought, and others expect you to act on all requests so frequently that doing otherwise would just be shocking to them. However, just because this is how you have been behaving most of your life does not mean that there is no room for improvement and change. Changing from an always answering Yes to replacing some of these Yeses with No answers is going to take some work, but it is not impossible. Somewhere along the line, you have to make room to allow for Yeses to things you want instead of always accommodating what everyone else wants.

Everyone Is Taken Care Of, But You

Have you ever taken time to think about all the things you would like to do but do not have the time to do? What about taking time to think about why it is that you do not have time to do those things? Although the answer to the first question may be quite frustrating as you think about all those things you wish you could do for yourself, the answer to the second question will be even more frustrating. While doing an evaluation of things you would like to do such as taking diving lessons, securing a personal trainer, or joining a book club, you may just realize how much you have shortchanged yourself from doing things for yourself. One reason you have not been able to pursue your own interests is that you have been too busy taking care of everyone else's needs to have any time left for yourself.

For instance, you are very good about taking your mother to the hair salon or taking your kids to every after-school activity that comes up, but you might not be very good at taking a whole day, or even half of a day, to go to a spa and relax or just read a good book. That is because people are living such fast-paced lives trying to take care of all their responsibilities that making time for themselves is almost unheard of. Often, due to such an ingrained feeling that you should put others before yourself, people put others' needs before their own. However, there are plenty of times when many of the things people feel they have to do are nothing more than responsibilities they have placed on themselves.

Consequently, as you go on saying Yes to your parents' needs, as well as your spouse's and children's needs, you leave less time available to take care of your own needs. It is easy to say, "Today after I get done with work, I'm heading straight home, and I am going to take some time to relax before dinner," but do you do it? If no one asks anything of you, maybe you will make the time for it. However, should you get a call from your brother on your way home that he wants to meet with you at the appliance store to pick out a new refrigerator for your parents and you say Yes, there went the time you had planned on taking for yourself when you got home. By the time you make that extra stop on your way home, there will be no extra time before dinner for you to relax. In reality, this is something that could be done a different day when you have more time, but instead, you get home just in time to take care of your daily evening routine, leaving you with no time for relaxing. In this instance, you end up going to bed exhausted, both mentally and physically.

What happens because of all this craziness day after day is you end up feeling frustrated and irritated. You are irritated because everyone is taking up your time with no time left for yourself and what you want to do. You are then annoyed at yourself and everyone else around you who might have contributed to your lack of free time. Regardless of the fact that, in reality, it is not everyone else's fault that you do not have this time for yourself, you somehow seem to perceive it that way. They might have been the ones asking for things from you and taking from your free time, but you are the one who did not know how to say No to them and instead, continued to say Yes. Just by doing a quick evaluation of the circumstances, you will realize that you are the only one who is able to bring some balance into your life. You must make time to take care of yourself and recharge your batteries, or you will have to face the consequences later.

Although taking care of your family's needs is important, constantly being on the go without taking time for yourself can lead to irritability or even exhaustion. Although people constantly complain of exhaustion from everyday activities, there is a more serious level of exhaustion — that of not only being physically exhausted but also mentally exhausted. When you put both mental and physical exhaustion together, you may experience a whole series of issues, as fatigue can affect all aspects of your life. It can affect your relationships with friends, family, and your spouse. Being exhausted can cause you to perform poorly at work, can hinder your communication and listening skills, and can reduce your concentration skills. Further, it has been proven that exhaustion can lower your immune system.

For example, Amber was a mother of four who was always very busy. Although she enjoyed her career as a teacher, when her third child was born, she chose to stay home with her children and took on the administrative end of the family's business working from home. Amber then felt that she had all the time in the world to do everything, and she did not know how to say No. She was actively involved in her children's school activities, her church, and her ladies' club activities and volunteered on a regular basis. In addition, because she was considered a stay-at-home mom and did not work a full-time job, everybody went to her when there were committees to chair, events to organize, or anything else that may come along because everyone expected her to have the time. What made the situation worse was she always said Yes, so a Yes was always expected of her. On top of that, although she had plenty of paperwork to take care of from home that was related to the business, her husband was also of the mentality that because she did not work a full-time job, she could take care of errands for him for the business on a moment's notice.

But what Amber finally realized is that even though she did not have a full-time job, she had less time for herself than when she was working as a teacher. She was starting to get sick more often and was often irritable at the end of the day. She resented the fact that she never had time to relax and enjoy doing things for herself. After coming to this realization, Amber decided it was time to learn how to say No and take back control of her life. All her activities, and the people associated with them, had taken control of her life. She started prioritizing what was most important to her, such as her responsibilities with the family business, the civic and social clubs she belonged to, the school activities she was involved with, and so on. She then evaluated how much she really wanted to be involved with each activity. She chose which ones she would remain active in and which ones she would just take a more passive role in. To her list of activities, she then added time for herself, such as time to go to the gym and time to take some personal enrichment classes. She also picked up a book that would help her with this undertaking and started reading up on how to get started. She then told her husband and children of her new quest to change and requested their support. Her next step was to actually start saying No. She started with simple everyday things, including saying No to things her children asked for that she normally would have said Yes to, and then said No to some of her husband's last-minute requests that she knew could wait. Saying No to those things alone started to free up some time for Amber, and she was not stressing as much by trying to squeeze so many things into her limited time frame of a day.

She started saying No to chairing every committee that needed a chairperson, to working the concession stand for every basketball game, even No to volunteering at the soup kitchen twice a week, and instead, volunteered twice a month. Amber's transformation was incredible. She was happier, more relaxed, and finally was able to enjoy the things she was actually involved in without worrying about how she was going to find time to accomplish all her other tasks. Although her change was met with some resistance at first, everybody eventually got used to, and enjoyed, the new, happier, and more relaxed Amber.

When you really think about it, it is not worth getting irritated and exhausted just to take care of everyone else around you. In the end, you might end up not being able to take care of even your most basic needs. You can run yourself down to the point where everyone else may end up having to take care of you, instead of you taking care of them.

Saying No to Your Children

Maintaining a happy and healthy home involves a lot of give and take from all members of the family. There has to be an understanding from all the parties involved that every member of the family has his or her own responsibilities. However, for some reason, there is always the one member of the family who seems to carry the heavier load by taking care of not only his or her responsibilities but also seems to pick up many extra responsibilities from family members. Especially in the households when only one of the parents works, the stay-at-home parent is the one who typically ends up performing more tasks around the house. This also holds true in households where there is a single parent raising the children. In those instances, the burden is quite heavy for a single person to carry.

Learning how to say No to your children does not make you a bad parent. In fact, it is actually a characteristic of good parenting, because when you start saying No to your children's requests, they can take care of themselves, creating a balance in your life and theirs. Parents get used to doing everything for their children because they have had to do so since they were born. The problem is that sometimes parents do not realize that as children get older they are capable of taking on more responsibilities. Sometimes parents just continue to do as much for their children when they are teenagers as they did when they were toddlers.

Giving children added responsibilities and chores around the house is a way of saying No to old behavioral patterns while teaching them responsibility and self-discipline. For example, your 15-year-old son is used to coming home from football practice and throwing his practice uniform on top of the washing machine so you can clean it before his next day's practice. As a parent, you feel it is your responsibility to make sure the children always have clean clothes to wear. However, there is nothing wrong with teaching your son how to use the washing machine and dryer so he can wash his own uniform. The next time he throws his uniform in the laundry room for you to wash, you should be able to walk up to him and say, "I have a lot of other things to do this evening, so I can't wash your uniform, but if you come here I will show you how to do it yourself." Sometimes children need to experience firsthand some of the many tasks that you do for them to appreciate all that you do. Just imagine what will happen if one day you get injured, and you are not able to get around the house. Unless you have taught your children how to do some things for themselves, it would be total chaos.

As children get older and begin to get involved in different activities, it is amazing the number of things they volunteer their parents for without having any regard for all the other things the parents may have to do — things such as carpooling for soccer practice, taking friends home from school, or even baking for a bake sale. It is not that they are being inconsiderate, it is just that they are used to you being "super parent" and being able to do it all. Nonetheless, at some point, they have to realize that you are not a superhero of any kind. Although it may be a little hard for them to fathom, there are limits as to how much you can do without reaching a point of total exhaustion.

For instance, on the way home from school, your 13-year-old daughter tells you she volunteered you to bake cookies for the next day's bake sale at school. It is Wednesday, and that is the day that you normally would attend kickboxing class after an early dinner, so you consider giving up your class so you can bake the cookies for the school's fundraiser. However, instead of giving up the class, you make a stop on the way home at the grocery store, get prepackaged cookie dough, and when you get home, you show your daughter how to make the cookies herself.

Saying No to your children's requests is not turning your back and letting your children figure things out for themselves. Instead, you are providing them with the tools and knowledge necessary for them to be able to carry out whatever the task may be, taking these requests as opportunities to teach them skills they will need as they become adults. Because parents love their children and get such a sense of satisfaction and gratification for all that they do for their kids, they do not realize that, in the end, these actions may turn out to be counterproductive. Sometimes in wanting to do so much for their kids, parents overlook the fact that they are raising kids who totally depend on others to meet all their needs rather than teaching them to be self-sufficient and independent individuals.

There is also the other aspect of saying No to your children, and that is when they are asking for new items, to go places, or do things. As much as you want to make your children happy, you cannot always give in and say Yes to their requests. As parents, regardless of how much you do for your children, sometimes you feel as if you are not doing enough for them. Yet, you must establish a sense of authority, thereby creating healthy boundaries while keeping your children's best interests in mind at all times. Learning when and how to say Yes or No to children is one of parents' biggest challenges. If you tell them Yes too many times, your children can become spoiled and selfish and expect to always get their way. On the other hand, too many No's can cause them to feel angry and rebellious. So, the answer rests in knowing when to say Yes and when to say No. Realize that when parents rightly say No to their children, it is for their own good.

Conversely, before you can learn how to say No to your children, it probably helps to understand why it is that you usually say Yes when you should be saying No. Here are some of the most common reasons:

Guilt

As a rule, parents want what is best for their children. Once someone becomes a parent, he or she feels it is his or her life mission to see to it that his or her children are loved and cared for and that their needs are met, both mentally and physically. Parents want to ensure their children's happiness, sometimes disregarding the cost of doing just that. They feel guilty about saying No to their children when they want something because, as parents, they feel they just have not given their children enough.

Parents can feel guilty not only in those instances when they cannot provide their children with all the material things their children may want, but also when they do not provide their children with the same freedoms that some of the children's peers may have. For instance, allowing your preteen daughter to go alone to the movies with a group of friends just because her other friends are allowed to go unsupervised might not be the best reason to allow her to go. Her making you feel guilty, as if you are the "only" parent who do not allow your preteen daughter to go to the movies with her friends, is not a good reason to say Yes to her wishes.

It is also very easy for parents to feel guilty in those instances when your children want your undivided attention, regardless of what you may be in the middle of doing. Say you are tending to company in your house and your 5-year-old continues to interrupt your conversation by bringing you his toys for you to play with him. Out of guilt, you interrupt your conversation multiple times to tend to his desires instead of asking him and teaching him to wait until later for you to play with him. Teaching your child that you cannot always say Yes to each one of his or her calls for attention will also serve as a lesson in good manners and having respect for others.

Avoiding conflicts

Nobody likes conflicts or confrontations of any kind, which is why people try to avoid them at all costs even when it has to do with their children. How many times have you just given in to your child's constant begging just to appease him or her? On top of the other worries and responsibilities you have to deal with on a daily basis, having a child whining away is one of the most irritating situations you can find yourself in when it comes to parenthood. Although conceding and agreeing just to avoid any further confrontations may seem like the best solution to the problem, in the end, it will come back to haunt you.

For example, say Andrew has a 14-year-old daughter who is constantly nagging him about wanting to go out on a date. Andrew knows that if he allows his daughter to go in order to avoid the constant arguments, he would compromise his ability to stand firm on decisions he might make in the future regarding his daughter's upbringing, especially when he has always made it clear that she could not date until she was 16. Thus, Andrew does not waver, and although the arguments about the subject might be unpleasant, he stands behind his decision and does not allow his daughter to date just yet.

On critical issues, it is better to stand firm behind your No answers and deal with some conflict rather saying a quick Yes and then have to regret it later. Children need to understand that there will be plenty of No's as they go through life, and that they will not always be able to get their way.

Wanting their unconditional love

There is no greater joy to a parent than seeing their children happy. If they are happy, you are happy. When they are upset, you feel it is up to you to resolve the issue. So, how does it make you feel when you have upset them by not granting something they want? It may feel as if you were doing the opposite of what you really want for your children. However, it is important to remember that although it may upset them, it is impossible to always grant every one of their wishes. They may look at you as if they despise you, and some may even scream the ever so horrible "I hate you!" But you should know that deep down inside they still do love you and that saying No is not going to be enough for them to stop loving you. Likewise, you know how much you really love them, and that when you are saying No, it is because occasionally you have to say No for their own good. They may be upset for a little while after you have said no to them, but they will get over it eventually and continue to love you just as much.

Although saying No to your children can bring about that fear within you that they may think you do not love them, or that you are not being fair, there are ways to say No to them that will diminish those feelings. First, be consistent. When you say No to something, stick to it, and do not go back and say Yes. If your 16-year-old son is not allowed to have friends ride in the car with him, make sure you do not bend the rules, and be consistent. That means he is not allowed to have friends in the car when he goes out on the weekends, and he is not allowed to drive friends home from school. If you allow him to have friends in the car sometimes and not others, he will not be able to understand why it is OK sometimes and not others. When you keep your response consistent, there will be no room for misinterpretation and the harboring of ill feelings.

See if there are alternatives to the request that will work for both parties. Sometimes when children make unreasonable requests of their parents, they may be testing them to see how far they can go before reaching the parent's breaking point. Although, sometimes those requests may not seem unreasonable to the children, they may be unreasonable by the parent's standards. By offering an alternative to such requests and allowing your child some leeway, the parent can create a better sense of fairness to the situation.

For instance, your daughter asked to go to her friend's Sweet 16 birthday party and stay for a sleepover. Although you know the parents well, you do not know all those who may be attending and feel a little uneasy about letting her go. However, rather than just saying No to the whole event, compromise with your daughter. Allow her to attend the party but not the sleepover,. Explain that you are concerned with the strangers who will be staying overnight and your concern for her safety. By allowing her to stay until midnight, she will feel that at least she won half the battle, which for teenagers is very important, and you would feel comfortable with the decision you made.

This example carries over very well to the third way you can say No while avoiding ill feelings between you and your children, which is explaining the reason behind your No. As a parent, you may feel that you do not owe your children an explanation or reasons for your decisions. However, just as adults feel they deserve a reason when things happen, the same holds true for children. Children are more likely to understand and accept situations if they know why the answer is No, rather than when the answer is just "because I said so." Referring back to the example above, if you take a moment and explain to your daughter that you are very concerned about her well-being because you are unfamiliar with those staying overnight, she may understand the reason behind your decision a little better. Explain further that if something were to happen to her, you would be devastated and feel responsible for what happened. In this instance, you daughter may not understand your reasoning behind your decision. Instead, she might believe you have not realized that she is growing up and may feel as if you are not giving her the freedom she deserves. Make it clear to her you are truly acting out of concern as a parent, and that, under different circumstances, the outcome would be different.

At times, offering an explanation as to why things cannot always go their way may not be an option, but when the opportunity lends itself for such explanations, seize the moment. Taking advantage of such opportunities will always work to your advantage in the end, as it will teach your children a valuable lesson for the future. Knowing when to say No to your children, even if it is not the easiest choice, is a great investment in the future of your children. Saying No when needed helps to create boundaries that will teach your children how to grow into mature, responsible members of society.

Saying No to Your Spouse

Unlike with your children, where you are the ultimate authority, when it comes to your spouse, you should be equal partners in the relationship. It is not like you will be teaching your spouse responsibility or any skills for the future when you say No to requests they may make of you. These are mature individuals who more than likely are set in their ways and literally might not want to take No for an answer. Saying No is not a matter of playing power games, but more a matter of being considerate and understanding each other. Too many No's from either partner said in the wrong way can easily create a very hostile environment, and that is the last thing you want in a relationship. You want to be able to have your voice heard and to be able to say No when you feel it is appropriate without having to be concerned about the repercussions your response might have.

CASE STUDY: SUSAN PARKS

Senior sales representative
Ocala, Florida

Saying No when she should have said Yes is something Susan Parks admits she does. Parks realizes that one of the reasons for this is that she makes her decisions quickly, without thinking things through and makes commitments for things which she does not really have the time. But for Parks, saying Yes to too many things has its price. She is constantly feeling overwhelmed and stressed because she has too many things to accomplish within a limited time frame, and she knows it will eventually take its toll. For instance, in addition to constant traveling throughout the United States as part of her job, she also coordinates charity events for organizations she belongs to. Although organizing and working on charity events is very rewarding for her, it is also very exhausting.

Parks says, "I often feel overwhelmed because I have said Yes way more times than I should have. I am working ten hours a day for the job that pays my salary. I put in at least two to four hours a day to help promote a brand (that hopefully one day will also be paying me). I put in at least one day of family time, either visiting or calling my elderly mom and my daughter (and her family)." All this, plus all of the other social activities she is involved with on a regular basis.

Her biggest regret is all the Yeses she said during her previous marriage. While she was married, she could not bring herself to say No to her husband because she wanted to avoid conflict, thus agreeing when she really felt otherwise. She would put his feelings, thoughts, and wants before hers, rather than considering herself at any one time. When she finally started to say No to his wishes and desires that did not agree with hers, the relationship took a turn for the worst and eventually ended in each of them going their separate ways. Although she and her ex-husband could not work out their differences, she learned from the experience and swore to never allow herself to fall in that situation again. She learned to value her feelings, needs, and wants, and gave herself the credit she deserved. Her ability to stand up for herself and say No to requests she did not agree with allowed her to make a significant change in her life for the best.

In any relationship, there are plenty of opportunities for spouses to disagree, including situations where by allowing the other partner to continue with certain behavior you actually are stating a silent Yes. Putting an end to such situations without letting them continue for too long is an integral part of a healthy, happy relationship. Allowing a distasteful or unpleasant situation to continue for extended periods contributes to creating feelings of anger, frustration, and total dissatisfaction with the relationship.

For instance, Mike and Sandra have been married for five years. During these five years, Mike has been going to the local sports bar after work with his buddies two or three times a week. At first, Sandra did not mind too much, but at times Mike's outings kept him out late at night, which angered and frustrated Sandra. Instead of bringing it up, she did not say anything and hoped Mike would pick up on her anger when he got home, ultimately making him see that Sandra did not approve. By not saying anything, Sandra was agreeing to this situation that continued until the time she actually spoke up and expressed her feelings.

So, how can Sandra tell her husband No in a situation like this without creating a hostile situation? The answer lies in how and when she tells Mike. Instead of starting an argument when he returns home one night or calling him in the afternoon and asking him, "You are not going out again tonight, are you?" Sandra should address the subject by stating how she would rather have him spend the time with her. Stating her No in a nonconfrontational way will be more conducive toward resolving the matter than if she was to be abrasive about the situation. She may broach the subject by making statements such as "Why don't we both go out and do something together instead?" Or "I really enjoy the time we spend together in the evenings. Maybe we can spend more evenings together instead of going our separate ways."

There are many ways of telling your spouse No that will help prevent causing any hard feelings or bitterness. Using the word, "we" instead of the accusing "you" in any relationship seems to have a magical effect when used in a positive tone. There is something uplifting and pleasing about using the word "we" rather than just "you" or "me." By using "we" or "us," both parties have ownership in the situation and become an intricate part of whatever is being discussed. It is very different to say, "I want to buy a boat," compared to "We should buy a boat." Along the same lines, it is very different when the partner's response to either of the above statements is, "No, you are not buying a boat" instead of "We cannot buy a boat at this time." Using "we" instead of "I" or "you" certainly softens up the statements every time. That does not mean that the disagreement of whether to buy a boat will end there, but it will certainly reduce the tension in the conversation when using a "No, you cannot" statement.

Also, as you encounter situations when you and your spouse are in a public setting and one of you wants to make a decision at that time, using statements such as "This may not be a good idea at this time," or "We probably should not commit to this right now" will convey the message of No in a much softer way. This also allows both of you to "save face" in front of others and grants you the opportunity to discuss the matter at hand later, in private.

For example, you and your spouse are invited to a meeting at a friend's house to hear about a new business program that will allow you to make money from home. You go to the meeting and listen to the presentation, and at the end, the attendees are encouraged to sign up that night without giving you an opportunity to go home and think about it before committing. Your spouse might feel that this could be a good opportunity, but you do not. Further, you are not ready to make a decision at that point but do not want to find yourself in an embarrassing situation by arguing with your spouse in front of others. Thus, you quietly tell your spouse that you do not feel the program is such a good idea for you at this time and that you would rather think about it and discuss it further before committing to anything.

On the other hand, when saying No to a spouse regarding a matter that is directly related to his or her family, you must take a whole different approach. You must be very tactful and thoughtful, because in such instances, it becomes a matter of feelings easily getting hurt. The last thing you want is your spouse feeling as if you do not want to spend time with his or her family. Thus, it is important to be tactful and thoughtful in the discussion process. Creating a balance by interacting equally with both sides of the family is important for the overall balance that must be maintained in a relationship.

For instance, if there is a feeling that more time is being spent with one side of the family than the other, resentment will definitely surface. This makes the task of saying No under such circumstances that much more difficult. For example, for the first five years they were together, Nicole and Stan spent every holiday at Nicole's family's house because Stan's family lived far away. Within the last two years, Stan's family moved closer to the couple, and now Stan and his family expect the holidays to be split between both families. Unfortunately, Nicole does not see it this way and insists on spending every holiday with her family, which Stan believes is unfair. So, how can Stan effectively say No to Nicole next time she wants to go to her parent's for Easter? Keeping her feelings in mind and how much it means to her, Stan can state his side of the story and discuss how it is just as important for him to spend time with his family as it is for her. He can further state that by not agreeing to go to her family's house on that particular occasion, he is not undermining her feelings, but rather taking both of their feelings into consideration.

There is yet another aspect to the saying No element of a relationship. Saying No to your spouse or partner goes beyond those isolated circumstances where the issue at hand is worthy of some extended conversation. There are those No's that need to be said in order to maintain a strong relationship that balances both your needs and wants and those of your spouse. Although not always the case, in most live-in relationships there is this unspoken division of duties and responsibilities, and as the family nucleus grows, so do the responsibilities. Unfortunately, though, for some reason it seems as if these increasing responsibilities seem to fall heavier on one of the two partners. This could be because one has more of a "giver" personality or because some assumptions are made from one or both of the partners as to who is responsible for what in the relationship. In any case, a spouse should never take for granted or assume the other spouse will take care of a task because he or she normally takes care of it.

A Yesaholic confesses: Jacob and I have been married for 15 years, and during all these years, I have always been the primary meal preparer. However, as the years have gone by, our family has grown, and we now have three children, all in school and participating in extracurricular activities. Because Jacob had regular office hours, he was getting home pretty much around the same time every day, which was much earlier than when I was getting home with the kids because of all their after-school activities. The problem was that Jacob would sit around at home and wait for me to prepare the evening meals. After a couple of years of living like this and being angry as Jacob for not helping me, I realized it was partly my fault for not saying something to him instead of assuming he would figure out I needed help. So, rather than letting this behavior continue, I put my foot down, and the next time I got home and Jacob asked me what was for dinner, I told him that this situation could not continue. Unless he started helping with dinner on the days I got home late, he could take us out to dinner because I was refused to start cooking a meal that late in the evening anymore. As a result, Jacob started helping me with the meals on those nights that I got home late with the kids, making the evenings at home more pleasant for everyone.

In a relationship, when one of the two people feels like they are getting the short end of the stick, inevitably feelings of frustration and disappointment will start to brew. That is why it is so important to speak up when you start feeling shortchanged and start saying No when unnecessary burden is placed on you, because, otherwise, you will head straight for a burnout. For instance, if you are the one in the relationship who is always catering to the other partner, then there is no balance in the situation, and in trying to get your spouse's needs and wants met, yours will go unmet. When the scale of responsibilities starts tipping more toward your side, you should take action immediately. If your spouse has time to go out once a week to enjoy a hobby, you should also have time available at least once a week to do something you enjoy as well.

Ultimately, the goal should be for you to feel comfortable enough to be able to tell your spouse that you "do not wish to," "will not," or "cannot " do whatever the request may be. Using the right words you may see fit for the situation when saying No to your spouse will play a significant role in the outcome of the situation. Keeping a controlled and softer tone of voice when making such statements might diminish the chances of a confrontation because a nonaggressive tone of voice will set the stage for a nonconfrontational No. Learning how to say No to your loved ones in the least confrontational fashion will always be the best route to take because you have to live with these people.

Learning how to say No to your spouse is just one element of communicating with your spouse. The fact is, the way men and women communicate is very different. This difference in communication and the way men and women process information can be the cause of many confrontational situations. In these instances, either party may have acted based on the assumption that the other party knew exactly what was meant, but in reality, they misunderstood what the other said. Men will process information in a more factual fashion, basing it around reasoning and logic, while women base their reasoning on emotions, are very sensitive, and place a great deal of importance on feelings. It is because of this vast difference in communication patterns that miscommunications between men and women are so common. Remembering the differences between these two communication styles should offer a step in the right direction to better understand each other. Although, these patterns cannot be changed as they are just part of human nature, being aware of these differences and trying to understand what the other person's words and actions really mean can make a great difference in being able to communicate successfully.

How About Your Family Outside the Home? Elderly Parents And Siblings

It is so wonderful when a family is always there for each other during the good times and in times of need. However, sometimes people forget that as much as you may always want to be there for them, there may be times when your current circumstances will not allow you to be there. For instance, it is very easy to take for granted that your parents will always be there for you and will drop whatever it is that they are doing to tend to your needs because they are your parents. As you were growing up, that might have been their main focus in life, but now that you are an adult and have moved on with your life, they have moved on with their lives as well. They have had to build a life without children in the house and looked for other activities to keep them busy. They might belong to a bridge club, a bowling league, or even neighborhood watch groups. They are not just sitting around waiting for one of their adult children to call them and ask something of them so they can jump right on it.

If you were to turn the tables around, the same would be true for the adult children who begin to build and live a life of their own, taking care of their family and all the other responsibilities that come along with being an adult. The only difference is that sometimes it is difficult for parents to let go and see their children as grown adults with responsibilities of their own. They continue to expect their adult children to jump on command and tend to whatever their need may be. And as any good son or daughter would, you want to be able to take care of every one of their needs, but it is not always possible. Saying No to a parent is probably one of the most difficult No's for anybody to say because it makes you feel so guilty when you do so. After all, more than likely you owe who you are today to your parents and all they did for you. They tended to all your needs as a child and even as you were moving into your adult years. Then again, as much as all that may be true, there are plenty of circumstances when as much as you would want to say Yes to your parents, realistically, you know the right answer is to say No.

Then, how do you say No to your parents? The answer is lovingly and tactfully. Most of all, you want them to understand how much you love them and that you would do anything within your power for them, but they must also understand that there are times when you cannot tend to their requests. Here are some good guidelines to follow that will make saying No to your parents a lot easier and without the guilt — or at least without as much guilt.

Is your No justified? When you are able to clearly justify in your mind why is it that you cannot do something your parents have requested, the No will flow out of your mouth a lot easier, and you will not feel so bad about having said No. Say your mother asks you to take her to get a pedicure because she feels it would make her feel better, and she adds that tomorrow seems like a good time for her. The next day, however, is not a good day for you because your son has a baseball game, you have errands to run, and you have other plans with your spouse and children. Your mother believes the pedicure is important, and she wants to have it done then, but you know that something like that can wait without causing anybody any harm. So, you tell her the pedicure will have to wait a couple of days until you will have some free time and will be able to take her. You can even add that you want to enjoy the time you will be spending while taking her to get her pedicure, and you do not want to rush through it. Doing this ensures she will not feel less important than your spouse and children, and at the same time, you will be stressing to her that you view spending time with her as important. Saying No to your mother's request should be guilt free, because you know that you are not jeopardizing your mother's health by saying No to the pedicure. By postponing time spent with your mother, not only are you able to do what you had planned on doing, but you are also allowing yourself time at a later date to spend quality time with her.

Be concise; do not make excuses: When you start making excuses to get out of doing something your parents have asked of you, you will end up getting all tangled up in your excuses, which will make getting out of whatever much more difficult. Parents have a way of finding answers and solutions to everything, so beware that whatever excuse you may come up with, they will probably have a solution for your problem.

For example, John works six days a week and on his day off he tries to take care of the "honey do" list at home. However, John lives relatively close to his parents, and John's dad, Don, is always coming up with projects to keep himself busy. The problem with that is that nine times out of ten the projects are too physically demanding for Don, and he ends up asking John to come help him finish the projects. Every time

Don calls John to come help him on his day off, John runs down the list of things he needs to do at home, which will not allow him time to come help with Don's projects. The problem with that is that Don then offers to finish John's smaller projects so that John can then come help him on the day off. The only problem to this situation is by taking care of tasks around his house, John can spend time with his young son, which is something Don cannot do for him. John realizes that until he explains to his father that he just cannot come over to help every time he has a day off, the situation will continue. Ultimately, John tells his father that he cannot go to Don's house every time he is off work because he has things to take care at his own house and would like to spend some time with his son.

Find alternatives to taking care of their request: Telling your parents that you cannot do something for them is usually not enough, especially if you have always been the son or daughter who accommodates your parents' ever increasing needs. As parents get older, obviously their need for your assistance will increase as well. If you are not an only child, and your siblings are close by, everybody can then share the responsibility so that you will not be so overburdened. However, when you are an only child, or you are the only one of all the siblings who happens to live near your elderly parents, their requests for your assistance can become overwhelming, especially when you have a family of your own. It is in situations like this that finding alternatives to their constant requests can be very helpful. Depending on the circumstances, it may help to suggest an alternative such as taking care of the matter on a different date when you have more time available or suggesting someone else who may be able to assist your parents. Finding alternatives to their requests will provide you with some relief while at the same time making them feel that their request is important.

Say Jason's parents are moving from their house in town to a condo on the beach. They do not want to make the move on a weekend because they feel traffic is too heavy then, so they ask Jason to help them move during the week using his truck. Although Jason does not need his truck for work every day, he cannot leave his business unattended during the week. To find a solution to the situation, Jason asks one of his most trusted employees to drive his truck to help his parents move and pays the employee for a day's work.

That way Jason does not have to be away from his business, his parents can get help moving their belongings, and they still feel that Jason cared about them enough to see to it that they were able to move during the week as they desired.

Remember you are not a child anymore: Once a parent, you are always a parent. However, having once been a child does not mean that you will forever be a child. To some parents, their children grow, move out, and make a life of their own but as far as they are concerned, they feel as if they can still control their children's lives as if they were still at home. Some parents even feel they should have priority over anything else in their children's lives, regardless of the responsibilities their children may have of their own. Parents who are controlling and demanding tend to make demands of their children constantly without accepting No for an answer. Once you fall into a pattern of behavior where your parent makes a request, and you respond every time, it becomes very difficult to break this habit regardless of how tired or worn out you may be. Answering your parents' requests because you do not want to hurt their feelings and at the same time taking care of your own family's needs may not leave any time to take care of your needs. As difficult as it may be, there comes a point where you must put your foot down and set your priorities, explaining to your parents that although they are important to you, and you will always do the best you can to take care of their needs, you are an adult now with responsibilities of your own. Trying to make your parents let go of such controlling behavior is not easy, but it can be done. It may be a little difficult at first, and you parents' feelings may get hurt, but eventually, they will come around and understand that it is not a matter of you not loving them, but a matter of letting go.

Beware of parents overstepping their boundaries: When parents still feel the need to approve, disapprove, or even have a say on every move you make, they obviously are overstepping their boundaries. Such behavior can be very damaging, ultimately causing issues in your relationships and personal life. For instance, in situations where parents want to have a say in each step their son or daughter takes in his or her marriage, such as when to have children, you can be sure there will be tension. A parent who constantly is wanting to impose her rules on how her grandchildren are being brought up unnecessarily create very uncomfortable situations in her son's household as raising the kids is a task for the parents to handle, not the grandparents. In addition to it being inappropriate of your mother to be telling you how to raise your own kids, you would be doing a great disservice to your marriage and children should you not discourage and ultimately completely stop this practice. There is absolutely nothing wrong with telling your parents that there are boundaries in every relationship, and that overstepping those boundaries by intruding in your relationship is hurting you and your family. Addressing such situations with your parents may not be the easiest thing to do but ultimately will help build a much stronger relationship with your spouse. It will also help your relationship with your parents, because when you are finally able to express the frustration you may feel toward them, you will then be able to build a more loving and constructive relationship with them.

It is also important to remember that you owe your parents a great deal and when prioritizing to whom you are going to say Yes, your parents should be toward the top of the list. Remember, one day you will also be an elderly parent who will need your children from time to time, and if the example you give your kids is that you did not have time for your parents, and then you can probably expect the same from them in the future.

Saying No to your spouse, children, parents, and siblings is not easy because of all the feelings that are involved. You find yourself not liking having to say No to your various family members for different reasons, but somehow, you manage to do so because you know that regardless of what happens, they will always love you because they are your family. However, it is a little different when you have to say No to people who do not have any emotional strings attached to you and may have an impact on your life, such as the people in your place of employment.

CHAPTER SEVEN

saying no in the workplace

SAYING NO AT YOUR PLACE OF EMPLOYMENT CAN BE A very tricky situation, and that is why it is essential that you know when and how you should say No. It is an issue that affects not only employees but also employers and those in supervisory positions as well. If you think it is hard to say No to your employer, imagine how hard it is to say No to your employees when you know that your employees are your biggest asset. Saying No does not always involve actually saying No. It can also be not accepting a situation, a request, or even a comment, which at times can be a double-edged sword. Depending on how it is said, you can be perceived as an employee who is not willing to give more than the minimum, and as an employer, you can seem to be a cold, non-caring boss.

As an employee, you want to work in a pleasant environment where employees are treated fairly and with respect. You are there to do a job, and you should strive to do it well, if you are given the right tools and support that will help you to do so. On the other hand, as an employer, you expect the best out of your employees — hard work, dedication, and loyalty. However, at times, employees are not able to live up to such expectations due to unpleasant situations they may dealing with at work. For instance, employees may be consumed by long hours, unreasonable requests by employers, rude behavior from coworkers and supervisors, and sometimes even harassment, all of which are totally unacceptable in today's work environment. Therefore, saying No to all of these situations is not only the appropriate action to take but also essential for your own well-being.

So, what often drives employees to just say Yes and agree to everything, whether they agree or not? According to Harmony Stalter, author of the book, *Employee Body Language Revealed: How to Predict Behavior in the Workplace by Reading and Understanding Body Language*, employees can be driven to agree because one of three reasons: groupthink, the fear of standing alone, and just indifference. Groupthink is when people go along with whatever it is the majority of the group has agreed to rather than stating their feelings on the matter. By agreeing with the majority, the person avoids being set aside as the outcast for not agreeing and avoids any confrontation with the remainder of the group for differing in opinions. The second one, fear of standing alone, is most common when it comes to disagreeing with what the boss has to say. Nobody wants to be looked at as the uncooperative employee who doubts the boss's capabilities by not agreeing with the boss. Some people may even have a fear of being fired for questioning the boss. Therefore, employees just agree with what the boss has to say and avoid the possible repercussions. Lastly, agreeing due to indifference is one of the worst reasons to agree. That is the case when an employee has lost so much interest at work that he or she becomes indifferent and simply agrees to things. That is not to say that the employee is a bad employee; it is very possible that this indifference has been the result of having tried to make a difference in the past and having been ignored. All these are nonconfrontational forms of getting by at work, thereby maintaining a comfortable status quo.

"But My Boss Does Not Take No For an Answer"

Some bosses just do not know how to take No as an answer from their employees. They believe that they got to their position through hard work, so they expect the same complete and unconditional dedication from their employees. This is most common coming from older generation bosses who moved up the corporate ladder through hard work and many years of dedication rather than today's corporate mentality where sometimes it is who you know that takes you places.

When you find yourself in a situation where you feel that your boss just does not know how to take No for an answer, take a moment, and evaluate the situation before you continue to accept what is going on. No one in this world is exempt from being told No. Your boss may feel he or she is above being told No, and trying to get your boss to be more accepting of the occasional No's from employees is something that can be worked on. So, can you say No to your boss? The answer is yes, as long as it is appropriate and done in a respectful fashion. Also, do not forget that every boss has a boss of his or her own, and in situations where you have negotiated as best as possible, and your boss absolutely refuses to take No for an answer, you can always consider going to the next level of authority. It may take some courage and conviction to take an unyielding employer and turn him or her around to where No responses are more accepted, but it may be worth the try. Standing up for what you believe to be right may turn out to be costly at times, but, in the end, it may also be well worth your run for it.

For example, David is the regional manager for sales of a logistics company. He pushes his employees hard and tries to keep the sales numbers up for his region. More specifically, he pushes his best sales person, Abby, to cover more area in less time, thereby increasing sales for the region. However, Abby has a family and does not want to be away from home traveling more than she already is, so when David insists that she travel more, she tells him No. David has tried everything possible to convince Abby to extend her route, including giving her a better company vehicle and added bonuses. David does not know how to take No for an answer, and Abby continues to say No. She knows what region she was expected to cover when she was hired, and she also knows that David is expecting her to go beyond what her job entails for his own personal gain. As much of an annoyance as it may be for Abby to constantly be telling her boss No, to her it is worth it rather than just giving in to get him off her back.

It is possible to say No to a boss who does not like to take No for an answer when you know they are being unreasonable. Unjust situations will happen in the workplace, as this is not a perfect world; however, it is your right to say No when such situations arise, thereby taking your part in not allowing overbearing bosses to overrun employees. There are more than plenty of opportunities at work that lend themselves to you having to say No to the one boss who does not like to hear it.

When you are dealing with daily situations where a boss does not like to take No for an answer, you have to not only weigh your battles and pick the ones you will actually fight, but also be ready to compromise on those not so important battles. Compromising is not always a bad thing, and sometimes it will provide you with the ammunition you need in future battles. That way when you are having a discussion with your boss over an unreasonable request, and you are standing firm behind your No answer, he or she cannot say then that you always say No to him or her because you would have had instances where you have compromised. Again, the key in being successful when saying No to someone who does not like to accept No's for answers is to be firm and not make excuses. When you make excuses, you will sound weak to people who have a solution or answer to each of those excuses, leaving you no room to get out of their request.

For example, your boss asks you to head up a new marketing program that must be up and running within two weeks, but at the same time you are also developing the marketing materials to promote a new product coming out in two weeks. You tell your boss that you will be glad to head the new marketing program he or she is requesting, but it will have to be postponed for a couple of weeks because you are currently working on another assignment he or she had given you previously and is due within the same time frame. Although you are being firm telling him or her that you cannot do it in the time frame he or she wishes, you are letting the boss know that you will take care of it, only at a later date. For someone who does not like to take No for an answer, it will be difficult to argue such response because although you have said No to some of the terms of the request, you still accepted some portion of the request.

Avoid Getting in Over Your Head

People can get in over their heads at their jobs for several reasons. One is that they do not want to say No to their employer because they want to impress their boss with their hard work, thereby hoping to be considered for the next promotion or increase in pay. Also, at times, people end up with more than they can handle because they may be fearful for their job if they do not comply with all of the boss's requests. This is especially true in today's work environment where competition is tight for just about every position available. Although getting in over your head with work is most of the time the result of trying to please your superiors, it can also happen when you are too soft hearted and agree to help your coworkers when they ask you for help. Taking on too much for any of these reasons might have its merit, but it is important to remember that you must maintain some balance if you are going to be successful at both work and at home. When you take on too much, it is impossible to give your all to each task you are trying to accomplish because you end up spreading yourself too thin. When this happens, the quality of the work suffers, and you end up not impressing anybody, ultimately going home in a bad mood.

CASE STUDY: MARTHA SCHROER

Human resources supervisor
Tampa, Florida

A busy mother of three, Martha Schroer has had more than her share of challenges while trying to juggle a home, a family, and a career. With two of her three children now out of college and on their own, Schroer's life is now quite different from how it was while all of her children were small and still at home. With only the youngest of the three who is still at home, her involvement with school activities is nowhere near as intense as it was when all three were in school. However, this does not mean that she now has more time for herself. All those Yeses that were said to the different committees, sports groups, and such have now been turned more toward her job, church activities, ladies' groups, and other activities.

As a professional with a great deal of responsibility on her shoulders, making Yes or No decisions that will impact her time greatly are common in her daily routine. At work, because she feels she does not have the time to consider a request, more often than not, she just says Yes. Sometimes, depending on the request and the person making the request, she may briefly consider the situation before answering, but often feels the answer has to be Yes, regardless of how she feels.

After having said Yes when she knew she should have said No, she then dreads taking on the task because she knows it will be like trying to accomplish the impossible. Still, not wanting to disappoint those who have asked something of her continues to be the driving force behind her constantly saying Yes. However, she knows there are consequences to her inability to say No, and unfortunately, she feels it is her family who ultimately suffers those consequences.

On numerous occasions, her having said Yes significantly impacted other aspects of her life, and as such, she has regretted every one of those. "There have been many occasions where I have deeply regretted saying Yes, but one that comes to mind vividly happened many years ago. I was asked to be historian for a group I belonged to. I said Yes, even though I had very little information as to what the task entailed other than keeping a scrapbook that was going to be entered in a competition at the end of the year. This was very time-consuming, having to attend meetings and functions all year to take pictures and notes. At the end, the scrapbook was due at a very busy time of the year for my family. We had multiple commitments, and the deadline was the same weekend as my daughter's First Communion, which required a great deal of preparation. My husband and my best friend were wonderful helping to complete the book on time so we could enjoy our daughter's special day." According to Schroer, that experience served as a valuable learning experience. Since then, she tries to find out more about requests such as this before accepting or declining.

If you really want to impress your boss with your work and your work ethics, learn how to say No when you are being overburdened with the work. The boss will more than likely appreciate you turning in quality work rather than a large quantity of work. If the work has to be returned to you for corrections and changes because it was done haphazardly because you were hurrying, you are being counterproductive; instead of moving on to the next project, you will be going back to fix your mistakes.

Say you are employed in the human resources department of your company in charge of all the hires, terminations, and personnel actions. Your days are pretty busy with paperwork and meetings all day long, but your boss approaches you and asks you to take on a study of how many workers' compensation cases the company has had in the last five years and would like the project completed within the next two weeks. You tell your boss you will take care of it even though, in addition to your regular work, you are already working on an employment fair coming up in three weeks. After taking a few minutes to think about all this, you realize that realistically even if you were to work longer hours and probably part of the weekend, it will not be humanly impossible to get all this accomplished. Rather than trying to accomplish the impossible, you should approach your boss and explain how you took a few minutes to evaluate your workload, and that it will be impossible for you to accomplish both of these tasks on top of your regular assignments. However, because your main goal for having said Yes to all of it to begin with was to impress your boss, impress your boss even more by offering some alternatives rather than just saying that you cannot do it. You can suggest something like putting a task force together to organize the job fair or assigning it to a less experienced coworker who will gain a lot from the experience.

If a problem stems out of your fear of losing your job if you were to tell you boss No, then you really need to evaluate your employment situation and whether the issue is a matter of fact or your perception of your boss. Realistically, if the situation at your job is such that people are terminated for not agreeing to comply with the boss's requests for additional work, then more than likely, people are terminated for poor performance as well. If this is true for you, determine from your boss what is more important to him or her: quality of work or quantity. Consequently, that is why it is so important to maintain a good rapport and keep the lines of communication open with your superiors, so you know what you can expect from them and what they in turn expect of you. If your boss makes requests that do not fall within your job description, are unreasonable, or even of a personal nature, you have every right to deny the request, but remember to do respectfully.

Say Bruce is going out of town on vacation for a week and asks his assistant Emily to take care of a couple of projects for him while he is out. Already bogged down with the extra work, Emily gets a phone call from Bruce on Thursday. He is asking her to go to his house in the morning and again in mid-afternoon to take his dogs out and feed them because the pet sitter had an emergency. Emily is already way over her head with work and knows she only has a couple of more days left in the week to accomplish all she has to do. To avoid further burdening herself, Emily tells Bruce that there is no way she can spare the time from work to take care of his dogs, and instead, she can get him the phone number to an alternate pet sitting service that could take care of his dogs that day. Emily needs to be assertive and not compromise her ability to complete her assigned work in order to take care of the boss's personal needs. Ultimately, Emily cannot get fired or reprimanded for not taking care of the boss's dogs, but she can receive some type of reprimand for not completing her work.

The situation is a little different when the person you have to learn to say No to is a coworker and not your boss. This should come easier to you because the coworker does not have any say over your job, but the truth is that people tend to be just as weak saying No to coworkers as to their boss, although for different reasons. There is that sense of camaraderie that gets you every time. You help them, and they help you. The problem is that, at times, you end up saying Yes to them quite a bit more often that they say Yes to you. If you start saying Yes to Tyrone's constant request for you to cover the phones for him, you agree on multiple times to review Michael's spreadsheets before he turns them in, and on top of that, you agree to help Christine with the company's monthly luncheon meetings, you will never be able to take care of your own workload. It is OK to help each other in the workplace, but it is another thing to be taken advantage of or to take advantage of people because that is not conducive to a productive environment. Next time Tyrone asks you to cover the phone for him, you need to tell him that you would but at this moment, you do not have the time to spare. When Michael asks you to review his spreadsheets, which is time-consuming, you tell him that you do not mind helping him with that occasionally, but you cannot take that much time away from your work to review his work every time he has a spreadsheet to turn in. As far as Christine's lunch meeting planning process, you might want to tell her that she needs to find somebody else in the office to help her with this monthly task because you cannot dedicate so much time every month to something that is not within your job duties. Although it is kind of you to help your coworkers, they are shining due to your help, while you are struggling to get your work done.

Learning how to say No to avoid getting in over your head will not only reduce your work-related stress, but will also help with your personal life because being stressed about work will affect your performance at work as well as your relationships at home. If you come home stressed because of all the work that you have to do or bring the work home, you will be giving up quality time you could be spending with your family. Then, not only will you be stressing over all the work you are doing on your own time, but you will also be angry and upset about taking the time away from your family and ultimately from yourself to do the work.

Working on Group Projects

It is very likely that at one point or another during your employment, you have been, or will be, asked to work on group projects. Although they can be interesting and challenging at times, it can become a stressful situation when the members of the team do not pull their fair share of the load. Some do less than others because their participation in the project does not require as much input, but other coworkers might try to pawn their share of the work on other members of the team. Unless you have the skills and inner strength to say No to these individuals who ask you to do their work for them, you are going to be in deep trouble.

However, sometimes getting overburdened has nothing to do with people asking you to take more on, but instead it is you not being able to tell yourself No — that is, stopping yourself from taking on more than what is actually your responsibility because you may be the type that likes to take charge of situations.

If the problem lies with being asked to do more by one or more member so of the team, then you need to work on learning how to say No to their requests. You need to be straightforward yet polite. You do not want to give them any negotiating room. For example, you can say things like:

- "I wish I could take care of that portion of the project for you, but I already have enough as it is."

- "I know you have a lot of work to do with this project but I cannot help you with your assignment and complete mine at the same time."

- "I'll take it as a compliment that you want me to help you with that, but I do not have time because I still have a lot of work to do before our deadline."

On the other hand, when problems arise from your inability to tell yourself No, then it is a matter of putting things into perspective. Nobody can help you with this but yourself because only you can properly identify your priorities. If you know you have the tendency to take on more than what has been assigned to you when working on group projects, make a conscious effort and set boundaries from the very beginning. Evaluate the assignment that has been given to you, and establish a deadline to get it accomplished, taking into consideration all the other work that you are responsible for in addition to the project. Unless you normally do not have much work do to, when you are given a special assignment, your days at work are going to be even more hectic and stressful. If you consider taking on more than what has been assigned to you, you will end up having to work late, on weekends, or bringing the work home, all of which you should avoid at all cost because of the repercussions it will have on your personal life. Keeping this concept very present at all times will help you to tell yourself No when the temptation strikes to do just one more thing.

Not being able to say No when you are working on a group project can have disastrous results because the whole purpose of working on a project as a group will be defeated. When a group is put together to work on project, it is normally includes people who bring different talents and skills to the table that when put together can successfully bring a project to realization. When you take on more than your share of the project, not only are you going to be taking on more than your fair share and jeopardizing the quality of your assignment, but also you may also unintentionally be sabotaging the success of the project. In the end, trying to take on more than you are prepared to handle is not worth it for anybody involved.

Listening to what others have to say at work, whether is verbal or nonverbal, is critical to your success. Not only it is important while working directly for your boss, but also when you are working in a team. The following excerpt from the book *Employee Body Language Revealed: How to Predict Behavior in the Workplace by Reading and Understanding Body Language*, is a great reference guide that will help you when trying to read your boss's and coworkers' body language.

Nonverbal cues **to use** when dealing with employees, colleagues, managers, and executives:

Nonverbal Cue	Meaning
Keeping direct eye contact	You are listening to what they are saying, or you may be confident in what you have to do.
Keeping our hands at your sides or in front with your palms exposed	You are open to what they are suggesting.
Standing with one foot slightly forward	You are not tense or intimidated.
Nodding your head during conversation	You are compassionate, or you are listening to what they are conveying, or in agreement.
Smiling	You are being cordial.

Nonverbal Cue	Meaning
Sitting upright	You are alert.
Only gesturing with your hands when explaining choice between options	You are exhibiting self-control.
Smiling less than they do	You are showing that you are professional.

Nonverbal cues **to avoid** when dealing with employees, colleagues, managers, and executives:

Nonverbal Cue	Meaning
Rolling, shifting, or narrowing your eyes	You do not believe what they are saying.
Furrowing your eyebrows	You are angry or in disbelief of what is being said.
Lowering your head	You are disappointed or insecure.
Sitting with your hands behind your head	You think you are superior to your employees.
Crossing your arms or legs	You are closed off to what they have to say.
Rubbing or head or neck	You are unsure about what they are suggesting.
Tapping your foot while they are speaking to you	You are impatient and just want the conversation to end.
Rocking back and forth fidgeting	You are no longer paying attention and are distracted.
Pointing your finger or pounding your fist	You are angry.
Lowering or darting your eyes	You are avoiding the speaker or not paying attention.
Clapping your hands slowly	You are being sarcastic.

Learning How to Say No When You Are the Boss

Whether you are a supervisor, manager of an organization, or the owner of a business, being responsible for supervising employees can have its very challenging moments. Although it is important to be a good and fair boss who is well liked by his or her employees, you might end up saying Yes when you need to say No because you are so preoccupied with wanting to be the "good guy." You may also not want to say No because saying Yes to things, especially in a work environment, seems to eliminate a lot of confrontational situations. In addition, when you are able to establish a good working relationship with your employees, morale is up and so is productivity. However, in the middle of any good working relationship, there will be times when you are going to have to say No to one of your employees, and you should be able to do so without fear of jeopardizing the positive working relationship that exists. For instance, reprimanding employees may not be the easiest thing to do, especially when you are new at supervising. Nevertheless, if in the process of managing your employees, you take the time to praise your employees for work well done, when you have to reprimand them for something, they will more than likely take it better than if you are always complaining about their work.

For example, Scott is responsible for supervising three employees in the graphics department of a marketing company. He has established a good working relationship with his employees and praises them often for their work well done. However, from time to time Scott's employees make mistakes that, should they go undetected, could be very costly to the company. Therefore, when Scott finds a mistake, he must address it immediately and stress the importance of accuracy to avoid such mistakes in the future. Keeping in mind that Scott praises his employees often, when he has to reprimand them, he addresses the situation by saying things such as, "Debbie you always do such good work, but in this case I cannot accept your proof as it is full of mistakes. You will need to be more careful next time."

There are other situations at work where saying No to your employees might not be as easy, for example when they are requesting time off, a raise, or even a promotion. When a subordinate asks for time off, as a manager or supervisor it is your responsibility to make sure that allowing that person to take the time off is not going to jeopardize production or completing a project, or whatever the end result may be according to your line of work or business. As in other situations, each case and each request for time off is unique and, therefore, should be handled accordingly. In those instances where you cannot warrant allowing an employee time off, you have to tell that employee he or she cannot take the time off. Telling your employees they cannot take time off can be a touchy situation, but how you address it will make a world of difference, especially if you make them feel important and needed. Here are some examples:

- "I know you want to take the rest of the week off, but if I let you take the time off production will come to a halt without your expertise, and we have a deadline to meet. I will be glad to give you the time off next week when this order is complete."

- "I understand that you want to take a month off to travel through Europe, but I would like for you to understand that I cannot afford to have you gone that long because your lack of input will put this project behind significantly, and we have a deadline to meet."

- "I cannot let you take Wednesday off as it is the day of the board meeting, and you are supposed to give a status report on your project. Maybe there is different day that you can take off that will work for both of us."

Having to terminate an employee or not being financially able to give an employee a well-deserved raise are both very tough situations for any employer. It is at times such as these that your management skills and your ability to say No while trying to be sympathetic are really tested. Nobody wants to be the bearer of bad news, and you would rather tell your employees Yes to their requests instead of having to say No. However, when you are in a management or supervisory position, having to tell your employees No from time to time or giving them bad news comes with the territory. The key to successfully telling your subordinates No or delivering bad news is to be prepared, to the point, and convey the information tactfully.

For example, Bill had been working for the same company for more than 15 years. He had been promoted three times during his tenure and eventually held the position of assistant marketing director. As an assistant director, he had to perform the duties of the director, David, on several occasions while David had been out. In fact, Bill had received compliments from management on doing an excellent job in David's absence. After years of working as marketing director, David left the company, giving two weeks notice and using the two weeks as vacation time. Over the course of one day, Bill had to take charge of the department while the position was being advertised, and the hiring process ran its course. As it was to be expected, Bill applied for the position along with numerous other people and was ultimately interviewed by Nelson, the human resources director. Nelson had seen Bill's performance through the years and was aware that he was capable of performing the duties of the position. However, the job description specifically stated that in order to qualify for the position, the candidate needed to have at least a bachelor's degree in business administration or a similar field. Bill did not have a bachelor's degree, and a couple of the candidates applying for the job not only had the same or better experience as Bill, but also had the degree the job description required. Nelson was faced with a difficult situation, as he knew Bill could perform the job but was lacking the education requirement for the job. He knew that if he was to hire Bill, he could find himself in a position where the other applicants who met all of the requirements for the position would contest the decision.

Having made a decision as to whom he would be hiring, Nelson had to prepare himself to deliver the news to Bill. He knew he was risking losing a very knowledgeable and valued employee out of disappointment, but he knew at the time he did not have a choice. So how did Nelson tell Bill he had not been selected for the job? Nelson started the conversation by letting Bill know how valuable he was to the company and how the company appreciated his work as temporary director while the company went through the hiring process. He then told Bill that the hiring process had been difficult, especially because of his skills and capabilities and the fact that he had actually performed the job duties without any problems, but that, unfortunately, they had to hire someone else who met all of the requirements for the job. Nelson then suggested to Bill that he should consider getting his bachelor's degree so that in the future should the position become available once again, he would then meet all the qualifications for the job.

In this example, the employer was prepared to deliver the news, and in addition to providing factual information, he was also sympathetic with the employee, thereby softening up a little bit when he had to tell this employee that he had not been selected for the job.

Another difficult situation you might find yourself in is when a subordinate asks for an increase in pay. If the employee does not deserve the increase, it is not difficult to tell them No. If they are making a lot of mistakes, are continuously late for work, or fail to meet deadlines on a regular basis, you can justify to the employee, and yourself, why you are not giving the employee the pay increase. On the other hand, when you have to tell your employees that you cannot give them a pay increase because there is no money in the budget, telling them No becomes a little more difficult, especially when the employee asking for the raise is a dedicated employee who has been going beyond what has been expected of him or her. In a situation such as this, you can say, "I am well aware of your job performance, and although you are absolutely deserving of a pay increase, the funds are simply not available at this time." You can also say, "I agree with you that you deserve a pay increase, but the company does not have funds for pay increases in this year's budget."

Learning how to say No to the different situations and people at work takes tact and confidence. You need to be tactful as you will be spending most of your working hours with them, and you want to maintain a pleasant working environment. Although it may take practice to be able to say No with confidence and conviction to people or inappropriate circumstances at work, the bottom line is that it can be done. When you are saying No for all the right reasons, you should have no problem building up the confidence necessary to express a firm No. Unfortunately, the case is not always that of having to say No for all the right reasons, but a case of saying Yes for all the wrong reasons.

CHAPTER EIGHT

saying yes for all the wrong reasons

THE PURPOSE OF THIS BOOK IS TO LEARN HOW TO SAY No when you usually say Yes. You are looking for ways to improve your life by not being overwhelmed with so many things to do. However, in the process of learning how to say No, it is important to learn and accept the reasons why you are constantly saying Yes to others while sacrificing your personal interests. Having said that, it is important to talk about how people sometimes get overwhelmed from their own doing. These are people who cannot bring themselves to say No because maybe they have some control issues they have not been able to come to terms with. So, they would rather be up to their ears with things to do rather than relinquishing some responsibilities or assignments to others. To those people, this is their opportunity to some self-evaluating, and if you fit in this category, this is the time to set yourself free from such habits and begin to learn how to say No when you would otherwise be saying Yes.

Sometimes you might feel that if you do not take care of the task no one else will. You may also feel that no one can do it as well as you can, and that is why you need to do it. What about that overpowering feeling that your way is the only way to do things and so you must do it yourself? There are also those who love to play the part of the martyr and say Yes to everything so they can play up how overburdened they are. Worst yet are those who like to boast about how great and wonderful they are, so they also say Yes to everything, only to be able to say they did it. These are all very intense and real feelings that people sometimes experience, and they think it makes them feel good about themselves, but in reality, all this is doing is covering up a deeper feeling of inadequacy. In this instance, people overcompensate by trying to be overachievers. When people build themselves to be so indispensable that they have to take care of everything themselves, they also are creating a situation where they are running themselves down with too much on their plates. Only when a person realizes that this is why he or she is always saying Yes is when he or she will be able to say No when it is not in his or her best interest to continue piling on the responsibilities.

"If I Do Not Do It, No One Will"

Many people feel that unless they take care of a situation no one else will, yet they could not be further from the truth. There is always somebody other than you who can take care of things.

For example, Madison is in charge of four barn hands at a horse-training farm. They all have their assigned responsibilities, and when everybody does their share, the work gets done by the end of the day, as it should. However, when the owner of the farm approaches Madison with a list of additional work that needs to be done, she tells the farm owner, "No problem, I will take care of it myself." Rather than assigning some of the additional work to the other workers, Madison takes on the new tasks herself and proclaims that if she does not take care of it, the others will not even bother to think about doing it. As a result, Madison often feels overworked and exhausted because of all the work she "has to do," when in reality, she does not have to do it all herself. Madison needs to learn that she is not doing anybody any good, especially herself, because, more than likely, nobody is impressed by her actions. Instead, upon being informed of additional tasks to be accomplished in the farm, Madison should gather her workers and split the list among all of them equally.

"No One Can Do It As Well as I Can"

There are also those who do not know how to say No because they feel that no one can do it as well as they can, and that their way is the only way. Perhaps no one can perform the task exactly like you, but there is someone who can do it pretty close to the way you would do it. If you have a hard time saying No because you feel your way is the best and only way of doing things, then you need to learn to evaluate each request carefully and make a conscious effort to determine if this is an instance where you absolutely cannot accept anyone else's work. Ask yourself, what will happen if this person does not do whatever it is exactly like I would do it? If the answer is nothing, or at least nothing significant, then it is time to delegate the task to someone else. If it makes you feel better, you can even suggest somebody else who you feel may be able to accomplish the task as close as possible to how you would do it. In this situation you would say, "No, I cannot take care of that at this moment, but Julian will do a great job with it."

Even though there is always someone who is fully capable of handling a situation as well as you can, there may be times when you may be left standing alone having to say Yes. You would be the only one there expected to say Yes, not due to a lack of capable individuals, but because you may have built a reputation in this respect, and nobody wants to step up because they are afraid that you may feel as if they were stepping on your toes. Upon realizing that this may be the case, it is time to re-evaluate the way you handle things, and the next time there is an opportunity, present yourself in a different way. For instance, maybe next time you are working on a group project, and they are looking for a volunteer to take care of something, you should suggest someone else who is also capable of succeeding for the task, thereby removing yourself as a possible candidate. More than likely, this will help set the stage for future instances.

Saying Yes To Be The Martyr

It is bad enough when you say Yes because you think that no one can do it as well as you can or because it has to be your way or no way. When you do things because you like to play the role of the martyr who has so much to do all the time, you really are doing a disservice to whomever you have just said Yes to, because, more than likely, they will feel guilty about having asked for your help. When you agree to do something for somebody, unless it is work related, you should do it because you want to or feel it is the right thing to do, not for self-serving reasons. The martyrs will take on one thing after another while feeling sorry for themselves because they just have so much to do, and then they make sure all those around them know just how much they have on their plate. People like this thrive on having others feel sorry for them.

For example, Amanda is a middle-school teacher. Her main subject is social studies, but she also volunteered to coach the cheerleading team and be teacher sponsor of the booster club. Amanda has two children of her own who are involved in sports in high school. Amanda has to stay after school twice a week to work with the girls in cheerleading, and once a week she meets with the booster club president to plan activities for the week. The two days of the week she does not have to stay late at her school, she attends her kids' basketball and football games. However, as full as her schedule is every week, when her school principal asked her last week if she wanted to head the school's fall festival, she agreed. In addition to that, she had already agreed to be part of her church's food drive for the holidays. Meanwhile, Amanda makes sure to tell everyone — the cheerleaders, school administration, booster club members, her church, and her spouse and children — just how busy she is. She is constantly making a big deal as to how she does not have time for one more thing and complains regularly of being so tired that she is starting to feel sick. Yet, she proceeds to take on more responsibilities.

Is Amanda miserable because she is too overwhelmed? Probably, but this is how she operates and probably would not know what to do with herself if she was not to be in a bind at all times. Constantly living under such stress is not good for anybody as there is only so much the body can take before it breaks down. The constant mental and physical stress will eventually take its toll, and she may end up sick at some point. What Amanda needs to realize is that there is nothing more important than her health. If she does not start saying No to some things, she may not be able to take care of her children and all the things to which she has already committed effectively. She must understand that people do not admire martyrs. Instead, they wish they would realize the damage they are causing to themselves and should take time to reevaluate their priorities in life. For instance, is working with the booster club or coordinating the school's fall social worth getting sick over? The answer is No. Is there another teacher in the school who would be willing to work with the booster club and coordinate the school's fall festival? The answer is Yes. In this case, Amanda needs to evaluate her priorities and eliminate some of the responsibilities from her life while making a conscious effort to say No more often instead of always saying Yes.

Doing Something Just To Say You Did It

Learning how to say No is not just about learning how to say No to prevent feeling overwhelmed with all the things you have taken on, but it also means learning how to say No to things we are not trained or do not have the knowledge to handle. Sometimes people get so caught up in saying Yes to everything that they fail to take the time to evaluate, not only if they have the time to do it, but also whether they are capable of doing it. Often in the rush of saying Yes to whatever it may be just to say you did it, you may end up committing to do something that you have no training or knowledge about, and you end up making a mess rather than accomplishing the task.

A Yesaholic confesses: Last fall, after signing up my son for the soccer league, we found out at the first meeting that the league had more teams than coaches, and my son's team was one of those teams that did not have a coach. So when they asked for volunteers to coach the team, I said I would. I love to try new things, which is why I am always volunteering to take on new things. Even if I do not have the time or the knowledge required for the task, I just wing it so I can say I have done those things. So, I took on my son's soccer team, and we practiced twice a week. I had no clue what I was doing, but I figured that because most of the kids had played before, they knew what to do, and they could teach each other. I figured I would be there for administrative purposes and to keep them under control while maybe learning a little bit about soccer myself. As the season progressed, and my team was not winning any games, it was obvious that they needed someone who knew about soccer to coach them. But it was too late because

> *I had already volunteered, and if I pulled out, the kids would have not had a coach. It was terrible that we did not win at all that season, and I felt awful for the boys, but at least I tried.*

In the process of Tim not being able to say No when faced with challenges that he was not capable of handling, he shortchanged the team. Rather than allowing someone who was capable of coaching to come forward and volunteer to coach, Tim jumped right on it for the wrong reason. He was not looking after the kids' interests or coaching them so they could win; he was in it for his own selfish reasons. If Tim reflected on the situation and looked at it from an unselfish point of view, he would realize that he should have never volunteered to coach the soccer team when he did not have the knowledge or skills to do it and do it well. He should have learned the lesson that next time he is in a situation where volunteers are needed, or if he is directly asked to take on something that he is not qualified to do, he should say, "No, I can't. I would be doing you a disservice if I were to take this on. I am sure there is someone better qualified than me who can do this for you."

Whether you are usually saying Yes because you feel it is your duty or responsibility toward your spouse and children, because you want to maintain a status quo at work, or just for all the wrong reasons, at some point you need to stop. Saying Yes all the time is not healthy and ultimately can have adverse effects in your life. Taking some positive steps toward learning how to say No and setting some boundaries when you are considering saying Yes will positively influence your life.

CHAPTER NINE

setting healthy boundaries

LIFE IS WHAT YOU MAKE OF IT. YOU ARE THE AUTHOR of your own story, and as such, it is completely up to you to decide when to say Yes and when to say No. Your ability to decide wisely will contribute greatly to your ability to live a less stressful life with more time to do the things you actually want to do, rather than doing the things you feel you are expected to do. However, it would also be unrealistic to expect anyone to live a completely self-centered life, telling people No to every request that will not be to his or her own benefit. Setting healthy boundaries and creating a balance between the number of Yeses and No's will be the key to your success and well-being. You also must set some boundaries when deciding whether to agree to something if goes against your moral and ethical standards, whether it is in your personal life or your professional life. As stated by Oprah Winfrey, "When you do not set healthy boundaries for yourself, you are inviting people to ignore your needs."

Setting Boundaries for Ethical Reasons

At some point or another in their lives, everyone sets boundaries as to what he or she will ultimately be willing to do or not to do in any one given situation. Whether it is a conscious or subconscious decision, it is a personal issue and everyone has his or her own reasons for setting such boundaries. Think about those times you have been faced with a situation you are not comfortable with and without giving it much thought, out of your mouth comes, "No, that is as far as I will go." Obviously, that means that whatever the situation is, you had previously set some boundaries for yourself as to how far you would go if you were faced with a situation such as the one at hand. Those boundaries are like the guiding posts that keep you in line and hopefully, keep you from making the wrong decisions when faced with questionable situations, both in your personal and professional life.

There are plenty of situations where you may be faced with making a decision involving an unethical issue. No one really knows what makes a person tick, or what may be the motives for people to act the way they do. Some people may be very well aware of what their ethical boundaries are while others find excuses, justifying the reasons for their actions to themselves and others. When you are asked to take part of something that you know is unethical, your immediate response should be No. When you know deep down inside that the request goes against your grain, you should not have a problem responding with a very convincing No.

Julie is one of several volunteers who work on a regular basis at one the local church's food pantry. One day Julie spots Natalie, one of the regular volunteers, loading several boxes of goods in her car. Julie asks Trevor, one of the other volunteers, why Natalie is loading things in her car. Trying not to be too obvious, Trevor quietly tells Julie that Natalie has been taking goods from the pantry on a regular basis and selling them on her flea market stand. He then asks Julie not to say anything. Julie knows it is completely unethical not only for Natalie to be taking the goods that have been donated and selling them on the side, but also for everybody else to cover for her. Further, Julie knows it will be unethical for her to keep quiet and be an accomplice to the scheme. Julie tells Trevor No, she cannot keep quiet, and that she will not be part of such a situation. Knowing that she can either side with her coworkers and keep a status quo, or speak up and probably have them turn their backs on her, Julie does what is right and speaks to the church officials about what has been happening, letting them handle it from there.

When it comes to unethical proposals in the workplace, you can never go wrong saying No. If you say Yes to something you know is wrong and unethical, nine times out of ten, it will come back and bite you. Although at times it may seem like it is uncertain whether it will be ethical to accept, it probably will be in your best interest to just say No if you are not sure. That would certainly be a classic situation where it is better to be safe than sorry. Way too often, you learn of countries where unethical behavior on the part of government employees or even political figures is so common that all parties involved accept it. For instance, in the shipping industry it is common to run into government employees in foreign countries who are more than willing to inspect and move your cargo out of the port and to its final destination expeditiously if you compensate them for their efforts. Failing to offer this compensation may mean your cargo can sit at the port for extended periods. Although laws, such as the Foreign Corrupt Practices Act, have been established to eliminate these practices, this behavior is still a problem in some foreign ports. However, in general, most people do not condone this type of behavior. That is not to say that this does not happen in more developed countries, because unfortunately, it does to certain extent.

For instance, when a company or even a governmental agency puts out requests for bids, the work available is limited, and the competition is tight, there is temptation for bidders to offer some kind of under the table compensation to those awarding bids. And the temptation to say Yes to such proposals on the part of those awarding the bids is just as common. It happens in the public sector as well as in the private sector, with big companies and small companies. It is up to the individual to be honest and say No to such proposals. In such cases, the morally and ethically correct thing to do is to award the bid to the best and lowest bidder. Should you find yourself in a position where you are being offered a kickback to conduct yourself in a manner other than honestly and ethically, your answer should be No.

Dealing and overcoming situations where your ethics are put to the test will redefine whom you are and will provide you with an opportunity for growth. When you stand up for what you believe in, and you say No, say it with assertiveness and conviction so that you will be sure to be taken seriously.

Living a Balanced Lifestyle of Yeses and No's

Agreeing too often to do tasks for others, accepting to take on too many assignments, and not knowing when to say No are more than likely one of the reasons why you may be feeling so overwhelmed. One of these is probably the reason why picked up this book. Learning how to say No is not about learning how to say No to every request that is made of you; it is about learning how to say No when you know that is the right answer. Learning this skill will create a balance in your life so you do not get overwhelmed. There is so much to take into consideration when trying to create that balance. Making a Yes or No decision may seem like a simple task on the surface, but often, making a choice is a gamble because you really cannot predict the outcome or repercussions unless you know what to expect based on previous experiences with similar situations.

Although responding Yes or No is not always a major choice, as this decision seems to happen on an everyday basis, sometimes the Yes or No answer may affect our lives on a long-term basis. Situations where you may have to do a little more evaluation as to whether to say Yes or No would be instances such as saying No to a project that does not seem promising. In this example, you might end up wasting your time and effort on something that is not worth it. The same holds true for situations where offers seem too good to be true. Although your initial reaction is that the offer looks like a good deal, when looking at the situation a little deeper, it becomes evident that it really is not as good as it appears on the surface.

For example, you get a call from an acquaintance that wants to share with you a new business opportunity that will ultimately allow you to earn up to a six-figure income working from home. It sounds too good to be true, but your acquaintance assures you it is a good deal. So, you attend the meeting you were invited to, watch the video, and listen to the presentation. The proposal sounds good, and your acquaintance assures you that you will earn that much income "in no time." However, when you start looking deeper into the business deal, you learn that to start you must purchase a $300 startup kit. You further learn that in *order to make money, you must sign up people under you who must then sign up another number of people under each of them in, and everybody must sell a certain amount of product to guarantee the income. All this requires investing a great deal of time and effort in order to make it work. Ultimately, this is not the great deal you were promised. Although this type of pyramid structure setup may work for some people, it just happened that it was not right for you.*

Try considering the following questions when weighing your decision between saying Yes or saying No:

- Will my decision benefit others as well as me?
- Will my decision adversely affect my family or take too much time away from them?
- Do I have the adequate time that it will take to accomplish this task effectively?
- Am I going to have help available, should I need it, to complete this task?
- Do I really want to take on this responsibility, or am I doing it to please others?
- Have I taken every aspect of this request into consideration before answering?
- Can I comfortably say Yes knowing that I will not regret my decision later?

As you go move through your regular routine, it is important to keep in perspective just how much time you are dedicating to each segment of your life. For instance, are you taking on too many responsibilities at work that are keeping you from spending more time with your family? Are you saying Yes every time volunteers are needed at your church, preventing you from spending time with your parents? Is your involvement with your group of friends taking up time that you could be spending with your spouse? People often forget to consider these important questions before acting. Instead, they almost automatically say Yes to everything that they feel obligated to say Yes to. People seem to be more inclined to say Yes to those outside their innermost family circle because there is always the feeling that family members will be more understanding when they hear a No, but if they say No to the ladies at the club, those ladies certainly will not understand.

One of the most common aspects in people's lives where creating a balance between Yes and No answers is so important is between work and your personal life. Too many Yeses at work that end up taking up personal time are Yeses that should have been No's. When you begin to compromise your personal time because you do not know how to say No at work, it is time to evaluate your priorities and start saying No more often. For every Yes you say to something beyond your normal workload, you are saying a No to something or someone in your personal life. Most great leaders develop because of hard work and multiple

Yeses that should have been No's. However, one must wonder how many of them have regretted all those Yeses later in their life and wish they could go back and say No instead to have a more balanced lifestyle.

CASE STUDY: APRIL COLTON

Pharmaceutical sales representative
Ocala, Florida

April Colton's typical day as a pharmaceutical sales representative starts early and usually ends late. In addition, her job often takes her out of town for meetings and training sessions. With her career taking up so much of her time, Colton still strives to make time for her personal life, which is not easy. Although she is still not as assertive as she could be, she is pleased with her progress in trying to learn how to say No because she is convinced that she used to say Yes more than she currently does now.

One of the reasons she attributes her progress in learning how to say No is that she finally figured out that the problem was her constant impulse to say Yes on the spot. Now, she asks the person if she can get back to them at a later time before she commits, which has helped her in cutting back on her Yeses. Taking the time to get back to people not only allows her time to figure out if the request is realistically feasible for her to accomplish, but also gives her the ability to come up with a diplomatic way of saying No, if that is, indeed, the case.

While her ability to so say No has gotten better over time, there are still times when she has said Yes when she should have said No. Sometimes she feels terrible about it, but sometimes she does not feel so bad. It depends on the situation and what she calls the "cost/reward factor." If her sacrifice to accomplish the task is made worthwhile by the reward of having accomplished it, then she does not feel so bad. On the other hand, if it took a great deal more work and effort than she anticipated, and she does not get out of it what she expected, then it, truly, was a bad idea to have said Yes.

Saying too many Yeses made Colton feel overwhelmed, and she said, "that is one of the reasons I had to finally start reforming myself." Before Colton started "reforming herself," there were several reasons she said Yes when she should have said No. The most prominent reason she said, "is the fact that giving/doing things for other people gives us all a neuro-chemical cocktail boost of serotonin, our 'happy-feel-good' neurotrans-mitter and dopamine, another neurotransmitter that gives us pleasure and is highly involved in the brain's reward system." Colton further ex-plains that there is a catch to this: When you say Yes too many times, you end up in a situation where you are under a lot of stress, and the stress hormones produced actually cancel out the benefits of the good neu-rotransmitters.

Having experienced the physical effects of having said Yes one too many times, she has been working hard on learning how to say No more often that she used to. She looks at what she has learned in the process as "ed-ucational experiences," and now, her saying Yes when she really wanted to say No "are getting to be fewer as I learn and grow from my mistakes."

When you make promises that you cannot keep and take on obligations you cannot meet, you end up letting people down. You disillusion loved ones, let down coworkers, and disappoint even yourself, which then creates a terrible sense of failure because you could not finish something you had committed yourself to do.

What people often fail to consider when answering Yes or No are the repercussions of their decision. Too many Yeses will create a life where you are feeling overwhelmed, tired, and stressed. On the other hand, too many No's and you may be possibly robbing yourself of once-in-a-lifetime experiences. There is no such thing as a crystal ball that can give you all the answers and tell you when you should say Yes and when you should say No. All that you have available is your experience, your good judgment, and the knowledge you are gaining through your efforts to learn how to say No.

Motivation and Self-empowerment

What is it that makes you Yes more often than you should? Most people would say, "I am a giver, so I do not know how to say No." Others would say, "It is just so difficult to say No, especially when you are expected to say Yes." And then there is, "I am so used to always saying Yes to others that I would not know how to say No." Take a closer look at those common answers, and try to change them so they make direct reference to you, rather than the person who asked something of you. Change the motivation for saying Yes to a motivation for saying No.

For instance, take "I am a giver, so I do not know how to say No," and change it to "I am a giver, and having given so much of me already, I deserve a much-needed break." Instead of feeling powerless in your ability to say No because you are a giver, empower yourself by giving yourself the credit you deserve. Say No next time you are asked to do something that will take away from something you want to do. If your reason for saying Yes is, "It is just so difficult to say No, especially when you are expected to say Yes," change your response to "I do not have to say Yes all the time, even if I am expected to say so, because I am the only one who knows whether I can meet such a request." Regardless of how many times you have said Yes to the same request in the past, you are always able to change your Yes reply to a No. Whatever the reason may be, it is your reason, and it is not up for debate by outside sources. Only you have the power to decide over your actions, because only you will be responsible for the outcome. Changing "I am so used to always saying Yes to others that I would not know how to say No" should not be so difficult to change to "I am so used to saying Yes to others that it is time I start saying Yes to myself as well." Why is it so difficult to say Yes to your own needs? It may be because of that old ingrained sense of putting others before yourself. However, unless you start putting yourself first and taking care of your needs, you will not be able to take care of those around you.

Getting motivated to change our old ways for new, healthy, balanced ways is always the catalyst for the path to change. Some people get motivated easily, either by outside forces or even from within. There are others, however, who need a great deal of "push" in order to get motivated to do things, especially when it comes to changing their old ways for new ones. So, what motivates people to change from their old passive ways of saying Yes to a more secure and assertive attitude of saying No when needed? Normally, people are motivated to change because of other people, because they wish to experience growth in their personal life that requires behavioral changes, or they are in physical or mental pain.

Motivated by others

Being pushed into changing is probably the worst way to try to change. Trying to change something you do not feel needs to be altered is going to create a great deal of resistance on your part, and it may make you revert to your old ways. It also depends who is initiating the push for the possible outcomes. For instance, if your spouse is the one pushing you to change from always saying Yes to others because he/she is tired of you never being home, it is time to re-evaluate the impact your excessive commitments has on your relationship. The last thing you want to do is jeopardize your relationship because you do not know how to say No to others. In this case, you are saying Yes to others' needs but not your own, which, in this example, is your need to have a healthy relationship. It is possible that your friends will encourage you to be more assertive because they feel you put everyone before yourself.

When your motivation to change is the result of some type of growth in your life, whether it is spiritual, professional, or even because of a relationship, then you, more than likely, will put the most effort in accomplishing that change because it is something you really want to do. You are not being told to change or threatened to change; you are determined to change because it is something that comes from inside of you. For example, as a single individual with no ties to anyone in particular, you are free to say Yes to whatever request was made of you. Whether the requests are at work or from organizations you belong to, you can come and go as you please because you do not have to worry about taking quality time away from a spouse and family. On the other hand, as you go on through life, settle down, and have a family, things change. You then may be motivated to change from always saying Yes to others to really considering your Yes answers because you now have other responsibilities and emotional commitments.

Spiritual motivations

Spiritual growth within a person is one of the greatest motivators for change. As people grow spiritually, they find contentment in nonmaterial things. They move away from wanting to take prominent parts in organizations or move away from always saying Yes to everything so that others see how busy and important they are. Sometimes, when people grow spiritually, being in touch with oneself, with nature, and all that is pure and simple becomes more important than pleasing others. As a result, saying No to the not so important things in life becomes easier. Saying No to chairing the school's silent auction — which is normally a high-profile task — or saying No to chairing your civic group becomes a simple thing to do. People learn to say No to things that do not fulfill them anymore, rather than continuing on to keep a façade. Most of all, they are able to say No to all those things without any guilt because they now have other priorities in their lives.

Motivated by pain

People are highly motivated to change because of pain, either mental or physical. When people are faced with things in their life that make them too uncomfortable, they will change. Whether they gave it a second chance because they hoped that it would go away or thought they could get through it, there eventually comes a point where people cannot take it anymore. This pain and frustration is what fuels the desire to change. People who are involved in physically and mentally abusive situations and cannot take the pain anymore finally reach a point where they say "Enough is enough. I am not having this anymore." Saying No to get out of a painful situation takes a great deal of self-empowerment and courage, but it can be done.

Self-empowerment

You are motivated to change, otherwise you would not be reading this book. Change is not always easy because it takes more than wishing to change for the better; it takes hard work and commitment on your part. Now it is time to empower yourself with the necessary skills that will allow you to take that crucial step toward saying No when you really want to say Yes and ultimately take control of your life. Self-empowerment is about taking control of your life with the strongest power of all — the one that comes from within. It is about living your life how you want it and making decisions based on what you want rather than on what others want or expect of you. When you empower yourself, you allow yourself to become the strong-minded, assertive individual who is capable of projecting the image of someone who is sure of him/herself and is not afraid to say No. Remember, how you feel about yourself is the same image that you will project to others. Being sure of yourself and projecting that image will command respect and self-assurance, making your No answers strong and powerful.

Self-empowerment involves being honest with yourself. It requires you to get in touch with who you are on a much deeper plane, examining what your priorities and passions are, as well as identifying your true needs and wants. How do you empower yourself to become confident and secure about saying No when you really mean to say No? Here are some tips that will help you make that transition.

- First, ask yourself what it is that you want. You will only be able to pursue what you desire once you know what you want. Do you want to be actively involved in every committee that you belong to? Do you want time to enjoy with your family? Do you want the self-confidence that it takes to say No to all those unwanted responsibilities?

- Take time to think about and evaluate what could be keeping you from getting what you want. Is it old ingrained notions you were taught as a child? Could it be self-imposed limitations regarding what you think you are capable of doing? Once you recognize what may be keeping you from expressing what you really want, work on those issues and resolve them. Only then will you be able to break the barriers that are keeping you from stating how you feel.

- Take a closer look, and determine if you like what you see. If you do not like what you see, then figure out what improvements are needed. For instance, if you see an individual who is unable to stand up for what he or she wants and lets others intimidate him or her into making decisions he or she does not really want to make, make it a point to work on improving that. Draw strength from that realization to better yourself and make the change you know is necessary in your life.

- Make a list of the top ten things that are most important to you in priority order. Then, make a list of the ten things that you have been involved with in the past that you do not care for. Once you have made your lists, take time to evaluate the impact that each of the items on those lists have had in your life. When reviewing the list of the things you find most important, determine those things that mean the most to you by deciding the things you want to be a part of the most. These would be the things you want to stay focused on, and where you want to dedicate your time and energy. Now, look at your other list, the one with the things you do not care for much. You want to say No to these things. Making yourself aware of those things that do not bring pleasure or satisfaction in your life will allow you to respond with a No a lot easier when approached by people who want you to participate in such activities. It then becomes even clearer in which situations you need to say Yes and when to say No.

- Build confidence in yourself. Look at yourself and see who you really are — a strong individual with numerous qualities and strengths. Think of yourself as someone who knows what he or she wants and where he or she is going. Think of how these strengths can help you overcome your weaknesses and give you the fortitude to make decisions based on what you really want rather than what is expected of you.

- Take that newfound self-confidence and project a strong positive image of yourself. Remember that how you feel is how you are going to act. Pause and think before you speak and act, and speak with confidence. It is a cycle: if you project self-confidence; you are treated as a strong, confident individual; and you will act as an assertive, strong, and confident person.

- Be positive and maintain a positive attitude. If you are a negative person, that kind of attitude is draining which is exactly what you do not want. Try to see the positive side of things, including the positive side of saying No to certain demands and requests. Optimism and a positive attitude will strengthen you and allow you to see things for what they are, rather than what they may seem to be on the surface.

- Take your journey of self-empowerment by yourself and for yourself. Do not expect others around you to change just because you are going though this empowering transformation. Although it may take some time for others to accept your new attitude and outlook, they eventually will adjust and, ultimately, come to appreciate what you have become. Self-empowerment is for yourself; so, do not try to change those around you, because it will not work. However, this transformation will allow you to deal with the individuals you meet in a much more constructive and positive manner.

- Take empowering yourself one step at a time. You did not become who you are today overnight. Your personality is the result of many years of outside influences taking their toll on you. So, do not expect to tackle this matter from one day to the next. It is like weight. It takes time to put on the pounds, and it takes even more time to get rid of it. If you do it the right way, the pounds will stay gone; however, if you try a quick fix, the pounds will come back. So, do not try to go for the quick fix, because that is exactly what you get — a quick fix that does not last. Take your time, be patient with yourself, and watch yourself transform, a little bit at a time, into a strong individual who is capable of holding his or her own. You will not only see the change in yourself but also in your relationships with those around you.

- Do not be afraid of failure in your effort to be a stronger, more confident individual, and focus on the desired result. Focus on what is it that you want to accomplish, and try to stay on your path. No one is perfect, and there may be times when you weaken and start falling into your old ways. As soon as you recognize the signs, pick yourself back up, and continue with your journey of self-empowerment.

Your goal is to ultimately visualize yourself saying No, having the inner strength and ability to confidently say No when that is what you want to say. The power of visualization is immense. Mentally seeing yourself as assertive and confident while saying No will make this kind of behavior part of whom you are. By doing this, when the time comes for you to say No to something you do not wish to be a part of or do, saying No will be an automatic reaction because you are familiar with the feeling of saying No. Even if you have not actually said No to such requests in the past, having visualized yourself doing so will make providing a No answer a lot easier.

There is nothing wrong with considering your needs first when making a decision. You are as valuable as anyone else, and it is important to recognize that and let others know that as well.

Changes in Your Behavior Mean Adjustment to Those Around You

As you begin saying No at times when normally you would have said Yes, prepare yourself because those around you will react to this new, assertive you. Some reactions will be positive and others not so positive. Those who want the best for you will be glad to see you say No to those things you do not wish to take a part of. Others who have benefited from your "always Yes" attitude will not be so pleased and will push to get you back as you were.

Fortunately, all your newfound No's will translate into many very welcomed Yeses because every time you say No to something you are saying Yes to something else. Think about all the Yeses you were so accustomed to saying to extracurricular activities. They all translated into No's to extra time with your family, relaxing time to yourself, or even to something of which you really wanted to be a part. The people who care about you and want the best for you will be happy and exited for you as they see you more relaxed and at ease with yourself. They definitely will be proud of you for having taken such steps and might even wish they could do so themselves.

The people to whom you used to say Yes most often to will be the ones to miss your old ways the most. For instance, your employer who was used to you saying Yes to just about everything and taking on every task that was assigned to you will definitely have to adjust. The same holds true for coworkers who would, from time to time, ask you to help them with their workload. These coworkers will now have to realize that you will no longer always say Yes. Even the civic and social groups that you belong to will have to look for new volunteers to take on some of the responsibilities you used to accept on a regular basis.

When you have put so much effort in pleasing others by always saying Yes, you want to make sure you maintain those relationships after you have learned to say No. As you move forward through the process of learning how to say No and begin to use it more often and effectively, let your family, friends, coworkers, and other people you deal with on a regular basis know that you are making a much-needed change in your lifestyle. There is nothing wrong with explaining to them that you are working on learning how to say No because you have become overwhelmed with too many tasks. When people are able to explain the reasons behind a change in character, lifestyle, and such, others tend to be more understanding and even supportive.

Why people may not be supportive

According to Randy J. Patterson, Ph.D., author of the book *The Assertiveness Workbook*, there are several reasons why people around you may not be supportive of your saying No more often than before. The first one is that people are not sure how to interpret your new self. They are so used to the old you that they are not sure they will like you acting differently. It is like when people get used to their old comfortable shoes. They may be worn and a little faded, but that is what they are comfortable with. If you replace those shoes without the person being ready or expecting new shoes, they may not like them because they are not the shoes they are used to. They will assume the shoes will not be as comfortable until they get used to the new shoes and like them just as much. The same holds true for the new you. As good as the change may be, they may not like the change because you are not the same. They will even wonder how this change will affect the relationship. But eventually, like the new shoes, they will accept you and like you the same as before.

The second reason is that because you are not behaving according to their expectations, based on how you always used to behave, they may think you have changed temporarily but soon will return to your old self. After more time passes, and they realize you are acting differently from how you used respond to situations, those around you will come to the realization that you have adopted a new way of conducting yourself, such as being able to say No when you want to say No.

The third reason those around you might have a problem with your new assertive behavior is that people no longer have control of your life. When you are always saying Yes, you are actually letting others have control of your life. However, when you start taking on only the tasks you really want to undertake, only being a part of groups you really want to be a part of, or seeing to it that your interests are included in any decision-making process, those around you no longer control your life. Allowing people to pressure you into doing something you really do not want to do gives them power over you. When you become more secure and make decisions based on what you want rather than what others want you to do, you are taking the control you had previously given them away and taking it into your own hands. People do not like that and resent it; they will most likely resist such change.

People do not like change because it represents the unknown, whether it is something major as taking a leap of faith and moving to a new place where they do not know anybody or the simplest of things, such as having someone they know well act differently. Your friends, family, or coworkers may even experience a sense of betrayal because you do not seem to be the person you were before — as if you were turning your back on them. People who liked you better as the "Yes person" are going to try and pressure you into your old ways — mostly because it is to their benefit.

But, do not give in because, eventually, these people will get used to your saying No and learn to appreciate and value you just the same as before.

Support Groups Can Help

You may think: Why would I need a support group if all I am learning is how to say No when I usually say Yes? You are not just learning how to say No; you are actually making a change much greater than that. In order really to learn how to say No without hesitation, it will take effort on your part to change the way you have always been behaving. Changes like that do not happen overnight. It is the same as a chain smoker trying to quit or a gambling addict trying to give up the habit.

For some people, making a transition from always saying Yes to learning how to say No may not be so hard. Maybe they have made the decision to change and have realized what constantly saying Yes is doing to them. Perhaps this realization is enough to help them learn to say No when they really mean and want to say No. However, there are others that while they may want to change, they just simply cannot do it alone. Sometimes it can be lack of self-discipline, self-confidence, and even lack of support. People in this situation will, more than likely, need an added push to get them to make the change. That is where support groups come in.

All kinds of support groups can help when you are trying to learn how to say No. Sometimes a support group can be as simple as a supportive group of friends who are behind your intentions of changing and are willing to offer the support you need. It does not necessarily mean that you would need to meet on a regular basis with these friends to discuss your efforts. It just means that you have a group of friends who are willing to be there for you. They can even be there as a sounding board when you are faced with a situation where you know you should say No and want to say No, but are tempted to fall back on your old ways and are about to say Yes.

If you feel you need something a little more structured than just support from friends, you can seek support in different ways. You can seek support by joining more structured local support groups available in most communities. You can also join online forums — blogs or chat rooms that address assertiveness issues, such as the "I Have Got to Be More Assertive" forum where you can connect with people from all over who share the same interests in becoming more assertive. On this site, people share their experiences, as well as give and receive feedback. The address for this website is **www.experienceproject.com/ groups/Have-Got-To-Be-More-Assertive/104850**. In addition to this site, you can visit and join a number of other sites and forums. Monitoring different online forums for a while before joining is a good idea to be sure you will be joining a group in which you will feel comfortable and allow you to get the most out of your experience. Numerous publications on assertiveness and self-empowerment available on the market also can be quite helpful. There are also magazines, both printed and online, that contain articles on self-help and always provide interesting ideas and suggestions on how you can continue to improve on your efforts. Some of those magazines include *Experience Life*, *Psychology Today*, and *O, The Oprah Magazine*.

Support groups will vary by location, and they do not necessarily have to be tied to traditional medical health care organizations. They can also be part of churches or alternative/holistic medicine providers. Here are some suggestions as to how you can go about finding support groups in your area:

- Ask your health care provider or doctor for suggestions. You can also ask your chaplain, spiritual advisor, or counselor for assistance in recommending an appropriate support group that will suit your needs.

- Check with your local library, community center, and place of worship of your choice for availability of support groups in those locations.

- Check your local telephone book and local periodicals, such as newspapers, magazines, and special interest publications for a list of resources.

- Contact the national headquarters of organizations dealing with assertiveness and self-empowerment for information on satellite operations in your area. One example of such organizations is the Self Empowerment Meetup Groups. This association has satellite groups throughout the United States and other parts of the world such as Australia and Europe. Through their website **www.self-empowerment.meetup.com**, you can find the nearest location of one of their groups.

- Ask other people you know who are working on the same issues you are where you may be able to find a support group.

Regardless of what organization the support group may be tied to, there are many benefits to joining a support group. Some of these benefits include:

- Gaining a more clear understanding of your situation and what to expect

- The feeling that you are not alone, and there are others on your same journey

- The opportunity to be able to be able to talk openly and candidly about how you feel

- Gradually gaining a sense of accomplishment, control, and empowerment

- Helping you deal with the stress and anxiety that normally accompanies change

- Learning skills on how to cope with the reaction of those around you

- Helping you adjust to your new lifestyle

- Getting advice on how to seek additional support, if needed

If after investing some time and effort in getting the help you need through support groups you still feel you need more help, seeking the help of a psychologist might not a bad idea. Although it is more expensive than any other form of support, the psychologist is a trained specialist who surely will be able to help you.

Blooming and becoming a more self-confident and assertive individual is an exciting feeling. It will open so many new doors for you that you are going to wish you had taken on this transformation earlier. However, changes do not come easily; they take time. So, being patient with yourself and those around you who are trying to take in this "new" individual is important. The new, assertive you who is fully capable of saying No confidently and without regrets is about to live a fuller life as a result of being more in control of your decisions.

the new assertive you

AS STATED BY RANDY J. PATERSON, PH.D., IN HIS BOOK *The Assertiveness Workbook*, "assertiveness is really a set of skills, not a type of person." Being assertive is one of the most important skills that you can learn that will ultimately cause a huge impact in life. Assertiveness can be learned, and learning how to say No is a big part of it. Learning when and how to say No is exercising assertiveness, which then allows you to take control of your life and live under your terms, not everyone else's. People normally are driven to be more assertive when they have a clear idea of what they want, such as wanting more time to do what they want. To be assertive, you have to have clear picture of what your goals are in life.

What is Assertiveness?

Assertiveness is knowing how to be tactful when handling a situation, while at the same time being forceful enough to convey your opinion. Assertiveness also requires knowing when to intensify your response when needed, as well as making sure not to undermine your input in any conversation by using passive body language. Assertiveness allows you to express your needs, wants, and opinions without hurting the needs, wants, and opinions of those around you.

Unfortunately, because of people's need to be liked, if their opinions and feelings do not agree with those of the people around them, they tend to keep their opinions and feelings to themselves. This kind of situation results in other people taking advantage of people who are less confident and more passive than they are. Being assertive will keep you from being cheated out of what you want and deserve in life.

Some examples of assertive behavior include:

- Being able to express both negative and positive emotions
- Being able to address issues and situations that bother you
- Being able to be firm so others respect your rights
- Being able to start and end conversations confidently
- Being able to ask your friends for favors without feeling guilty
- Being able to express your opinions, feelings, and needs to those around you
- Questioning things that do not seem right to you
- Being able to say No

> *For instance, you are in line at the grocery store and somebody gets in front of you. Being an assertive individual, you would say in a polite manner "Excuse me. I guess you did not see me, but I was in line first. Can you please step back?" In this situation, you were polite but firm. Had you not been confident or assertive enough, you probably would have just let the person cut in front of you and not have said a word.*

Another good tool to remember when being assertive is to begin your answer with the word No because it states a firm answer from the start. Here are some examples of assertive No answers:

- "Angie, can you coordinate this year's United Way Campaign?" *"No, I have too many other commitments at the time; maybe you can find somebody else."*

- "Julio, can I borrow your motorcycle this weekend while you are out of town?" *"No, there is too much liability, and I do not want to take a chance."*

- "Andy, can you cosign on a bank loan for me to buy a car?" *"No, I have a policy of not cosigning for anybody."*

- "Bonnie, will you watch my dogs for me this weekend?" *"No, I can't. I have a basketball tournament to go to."*

How Can I Become More Assertive?

To become more assertive, you have to want to become a confident, assertive individual. You either are assertive, or you are not; there is no such thing as an in-between. You have to really want it and follow through until you reach your goal. One of the main things to address when you are trying to become more assertive is to become a good communicator. It is important that you are able to communicate exactly what you intended, so your statement is not misconstrued, which can not only send the wrong information, but also the wrong impression. Using the wrong words to communicate what you are trying to say can result in misunderstandings and confusion for all parties involved.

For instance, Mike, the project manager at a consulting firm, asks one of the team members, Tom, to take on the new account the company just picked up. As it is, Tom is totally overwhelmed with work and knows he just cannot pick up one more account. However, not being an assertive person, Tom tells Mike, "I do not think I can with all these other accounts I currently have. I am not sure I have the extra time available to handle one new account." Because Tom did not communicate clearly that he could not take on the new account, Mike's perception was that that he did not outright say No, so Mike tells Tom, "Oh, don't worry, you can handle it, you always can. I will have the file on your desk late this afternoon."

In this particular scenario, the key phrases that communicated the wrong information were "I do not think I can," and "I am not sure." These two phrases are clear indicators of non-assertiveness. Tom's response should have been "Mike, I cannot take on the new account as I will not be able to dedicate to it the time and effort it needs. I suggest you give the new account to Andrew, who is currently only handling one account."

Being a good listener is also as important in being assertive as being a good communicator. When you are assertive, you listen intently to what is being said to you so that you have a clear understanding of what is being communicated. If you do not understand clearly what was said or if you have a question about what was said, it is important that you ask and get clarification. When you do not ask for clarification, you may end up saying Yes to something that you would have rather said No to.

For example, Tara, one of the parents in a car pooling group, calls Sandra mid-morning and asks her if she could take care of the car pool next time because she has a doctor's appointment. Instead of asking if "next time" meant that afternoon's pickup or the following week, Sandra says Yes and hung up. Sandra assumed that Tara had meant filling in for her turn next week, so Sandra kept her hair appointment for that afternoon, planning to be home just in time for the kids to be dropped off. However, to Sandra's surprise,

> *30 minutes after school is out, she gets a frantic call from Tara wanting to know where she was because she had not picked up the kids. Had Sandra taken the time to ask for clarification as to what Tara really meant by "next time," the unpleasant situation would have been avoided.*

Being assertive enough to ask for clarification is important because not everyone has good communications skills. If you want to stay on top of things, it is up to you to make sure you are always clear as to what is being asked of you.

In addition to being a good communicator and listener, here are some steps that you can to help you become more assertive. Putting these steps into motion regularly will help you become a more confident, assertive individual. Remember that it would be unrealistic to expect to achieve such change overnight, but it is achievable within a reasonable amount of time.

- Give yourself the value you deserve, and accept that you have every right to have your needs and wants met.

- Stand up for your beliefs, and feel free to express your opinions, feelings, ideas, needs, and thoughts to others with respect.

- Do not ever be afraid to say No. If someone asks something of you that you are not comfortable with, do not have time for, or simply do not agree with, you have the right to say No.

- Learn to deal with situations that may seem difficult at the time they present themselves, rather than waiting — because you are afraid to deal with them — until the situation becomes a crisis. Waiting for the situation to resolve itself or go away because you are afraid to deal with it will only make the situation worse. For instance, say you have a coworker who is constantly putting you down and belittling you. Instead of putting a stop to it because you are hoping it will just go away, you allow this coworker to continue this behavior, which only continues to get worse. Still, as miserable as you are, you do nothing because you are afraid to bring it up to a supervisor, which will then result in confrontation that makes you terribly uncomfortable. The solution to the problem would be to let the coworker know immediately the comments are out of place and unwelcome, and that you will not allow the situation to continue. You inform the coworker that unless he or she stops, you will report the situation to your superiors. This may just stop the situation right there, and rather than being uncomfortable because of the insults, you are only uncomfortable once when you address the situation with the coworker.

- Be open-minded to the opinions and arguments of others, and be willing to compromise as long as you feel certain that your needs and wants will be met.

- Respect and value the rights of others the same as you want others to respect and value your rights.

- Always, *always* communicate confidence and self-control. Do this by creating an assertive image with your posture, facial expression, and direct eye contact.

- Practice your assertive attitude, not only in real life situations, but also at home in front of a mirror. Practice assertive body language such as holding your head up high, assertive facial expressions such as keeping eye contact, and even assertive statements.

A Yesaholic confesses: "During my years in college, I was a member of a fraternity. The first year I was a member, I was volunteered to take charge and coordinate our fraternity's participation during Greek Week at the university. Not being assertive enough to say No because I did not think I had the knowledge or experience to handle such events, I did not even ask what the responsibility entailed. I was not until I started working on this project that I learned about all the meetings I had to attend, all the coordination of different subcommittees I had to perform, and all the hours I was going to have to invest. Needless to say, due to my lack of assertiveness to just say No, the quality of my work suffered as well as my performance with my school work."

Body Language That Projects Assertiveness

There is an old proverb that says that actions speak louder than words. This is very true, as you can be saying one thing while your body language is saying another, and nine times out of ten, what is actually being communicated is what your body language is saying. Body language is the unspoken form of communication everyone uses in everyday life. Body language has a more powerful effect than anything you might have said aloud. Studies have shown that 93 percent of people's everyday communication is through body language or nonverbal communication. You tell people more with your body language than what you communicate with your spoken words.

> *For instance, a coworker approaches you during your lunch break and asks you if you want to join her and a group of her friends to go out on her boat on Saturday. You slouch your shoulders and start looking all around, as if you were looking for answers, and then respond by saying "Well, thank you, but I think I have other plans." Although you are telling your coworker that you cannot go, your body language lacks assertiveness and fails to project your answer with conviction.*

The assertive way of responding would have been to be up front and tell your coworker "No, thank you, but I do not like going on boat rides. Next time you and your friends are doing something other than going on the boat, let me know, and maybe I will join you then."

Projecting an assertive self takes practice, but it can be accomplished successfully if you really put your mind and enough effort into it. Here are some key elements of assertive body language that will be helpful in developing your own assertive way of expressing yourself.

Eye contact

First, make and maintain eye contact. There is nothing that says, "I am sure of what I am saying" more than eye contact. Maintaining eye contact also demonstrates respect and interest on your part on what is being said. If you start looking around while holding a conversation with somebody, it just makes it appear as if you are disinterested in what they have to say and makes it seem like you have a lack of respect. The person who is constantly checking their phone, looking at their watch, or looking around the room while in a conversation gives the impression that they have something better to do or somewhere else to be than where they are right now. Also, the person who looks down while holding a conversation with somebody else gives out the impression of being shy, withdrawn, or even deceitful.

Distance

The distance that you keep between you and the person you are speaking with has a significant impact on how the other person may perceive you. For instance, if you stand too far from the person, they may perceive you as standoffish. However, if you stand too close, the other person may perceive you as pushy or aggressive. If you lean toward the person or group of people when speaking to others, more than likely, they will see you as a friendly individual. On the other hand, if you lean away from people as you are holding a conversation, they may see you as unfriendly and distant.

Posture

Maintaining the proper posture also communicates a great deal of unspoken information. Here are some tips on posture that projects an assertive attitude:

- Maintain a straight back and hold shoulders back.

- Hold your head up high at all times.

- Keep your hands down by your sides. Do not put your hands around your back as this projects a timid and insecure image, and do not cross your arms, as this may come across as not wanting to listen to what is being said or having a defensive attitude.

- Position your feet flat on the ground, shoulders apart.

Handshake

A good assertive handshake is firm, but not too tight. A handshake where you squeeze the other person's hand too tight might be perceived as an act of trying to state who has the upper hand. On the other hand, a "dead fish" handshake is often perceived as the individual being shy, passive, or intimidated.

How to be Assertive Without Being Perceived as Aggressive

As stated by author Sharon Anthony Bower, "The basic difference between being assertive and being aggressive is how our words and behavior affect the rights and well-being of others." An assertive person is respected and even admired, but an aggressive person does not gain anyone's respect and is avoided if possible. Although there may seem to be a fine line between being assertive and being aggressive, there really is not. Unfortunately, there seems to be the misconception that if you are more forceful than you used to be, you might have become aggressive. There is a big difference between being assertive and being aggressive. For instance, assertive people can state their opinion and remain respectful of others. Aggressive people ignore, and sometimes attack, other people's opinions in an effort to make their opinions seem to be the correct one.

In the following example, the individual was able to assert himself and say No without being aggressive.

Jason was on the market for a used vehicle less than two years old with low mileage. As he worked his way through various used car dealers, he was able look around, make price comparisons, and evaluate financing options. After spending considerable time in a large, used car dealership, he narrowed down his choice to two cars. Both were last year's models, had about the same amount of mileage, but one was considerably more than the other. Upon making his decision to buy the one that cost the least, he found himself dealing with a salesman who insisted on his buying the most expensive model. Jason knew he had to be firm and assertive if he was going be able to finalize the purchase without being there all afternoon arguing with the salesman. So Jason finally looked at the salesman in the eyes, planted his feet flat on the ground, and said to him, "I appreciate your looking out for my interests, but I will not buy the $46,000 vehicle. I am here to purchase the $35,000 vehicle. If you cannot help me with this transaction, I am sure there are other sales representatives in the dealership who will be glad to assist me." The sales associate was then more than happy to sell Jason the $35,000 vehicle.

As you can see, Jason was not aggressive or rude. He was assertive in his body language and verbal expression. He looked at the salesman in the eyes, assumed an assertive posture, and went straight to the point.

A comparison of assertive behavior versus aggressive behavior may serve as a good guideline of how to conduct yourself in different circumstances so that you project the appropriate behavior you want to be perceived by others.

Assertive Behavior	Aggressive Behavior
Speaks openly	Interrupts and talks over other people
Speaks at an adequate tone of voice	Speaks louder than the others
Makes eye contact, and maintains it	Stares at the other person
Stands with a relaxed but assertive posture	Stands very rigid during conversations
Participates in group conversation	Takes control of conversations
Values other people as well as him/herself	Values him or herself more than other people
Speaks to the point	Only takes him or herself into consideration
Tries to be fair and not hurt anyone	Hurts people to avoid being hurt him or herself
Sets and reaches goals while being fair to others	Hurts others in the process of reaching goals

It Is All About Attitude

Winston Churchill once said, "Attitude is a little thing that makes a big difference." Your success in becoming a more assertive person and being able to say No has a lot to do with your attitude. Remember that attitude is one of those aspects about yourself where you are totally in control. You can choose to let people run you down and make you feel like you are incapable of accomplishing anything, or you can have a positive attitude, be confident that the world is yours for the taking, and that you can accomplish anything you set yourself to accomplish. If learning how to say No after saying Yes all these years is your goal, then set your mind to it, and have the positive attitude to ensure you will succeed.

Anybody is capable of having a good positive attitude; you just have to want it and work on it on a daily basis. When you are trying to become assertive enough that you feel comfortable saying No any time you see fit, the best way to stay on track is to adopt the following attitude:

- Establish attainable goals so that you can experience success, not failure.

  Example: As you begin on your path of learning how to say No, set a goal that first week that you will say No to one to two requests that week.

- Stop justifying why you cannot become assertive by making statements such as "I was just born that way," "I am too shy," "I'm not strong enough of a person to accomplish that," and similar statements.

  Example: Next time the thought comes to mind that "I was just born that way," immediately counteract that thought by saying to yourself, "I might have been born that way, but that does not mean I have to stay that way."

- Make a choice that will guide you in the right direction toward success and will allow you to better yourself.

  Example: When faced with challenges, make a choice that you know will be for your own good. It may not be the easiest route to take, but worth it in the end.

- Start fresh every day, and take each day one day at a time.

  Example: Start every day with the mindset that today will be better than yesterday and an opportunity to build on what you started yesterday.

- There will be days where you will fall into your old habits, but all you have to do is remember to start anew. As long as you recognize that you have fallen and you get back on the road to progress, that is success in itself.

  Example: You have been following a strict diet and have successfully lost weight. One day, however, you splurge and have dessert with your friend. There is nothing wrong with that as long as you recognize you wavered some, but keep that in mind, and go back to eating healthy following your diet.

- Do not let your fear of the unknown stop you. Your not knowing how others will perceive your new attitude or accept the new you should not stop you from trying to better yourself.

Example: Take that bold step and say No to someone you never before dreamed you would be able to say No to, and wait for a reaction. You may just be pleasantly surprised to find that the response was not what you expected.

- Leave the past behind you, live the present, and look forward to tomorrow.

  Example: As long as you keep carrying the baggage of how difficult it has always been for you to say No, it will be difficult to break away and start saying No. Remember that any day is a good day to start saying No, and you will continue to practice this on the days that follow.

- Never stop trying.

  Example: The last thing you should lose is hope. So, if you failed at your attempt to say No this time, try again until you get it.

A positive attitude will take you a long way in life, but even more so when you are trying to accomplish something that takes time and commitment. The desire and good intentions alone are not enough to make a change, but adding a positive attitude will make a world of difference. Think about it. Having a positive attitude entails having thoughts and values that look for the good in things. It requires having the outlook in life that nothing is impossible, that problems and obstacles can be overcome, and that there is an opportunity for a good outcome in every situation. Most important, be of the mindset that for every door that closes, there are many other doors full of opportunities waiting for you to open them. Having a positive attitude gives you the amazing power to succeed in difficult situations.

Of all the people you know, how many of those people have a good attitude and seem to be successful and happy? More than likely, all those with a good attitude seemed to be happier and content with their lives than those with a bad attitude. Your attitude will set the tone for how you will see and perceive things. Although you may feel that you need to become more assertive and learn how to say No because you are tired of people taking advantage of you, if you have a bad attitude about it, it will be more difficult for you to make the change. On the other hand, if you decide that you need to empower yourself and learn how to say No and you commence your journey to change with a positive attitude, you will be successful and feel good about it. A bad attitude toward change will make it almost a painful experience.

The following are some suggestions about staying positive:

- Look at yourself, and accept yourself for the amazing person you are. Although everyone is very quick to point out to that nobody is perfect, you need to take time to assess yourself and realize all your wonderful attributes. Play down your weaknesses, and play up your strengths.

- When you get up, make it your choice to have a good day. If you get up and say: "Boy, this is going to be one tough day"; you have predisposed yourself to having such a day. However, should you get up and say: "This is going to be a great day. One more day of success toward achieving my goal of learning how to say No when I know that is what I want to say." You will have that kind of day. Regardless of what happens, mentally, you have prepared yourself to have a successful day, and even during challenging situations, you will see the good side of things and not worry about the minor problems.

- Visualize yourself having an amazing and successful day. A key factor to a positive attitude is self-visualization. Visualizing success in attaining your goals makes you feel at ease and comfortable with whatever it is that you are attempting to achieve in your life, whether it is a tangible thing or attaining goals you have set for yourself such as making changes in how and when you say No.

- Be enthusiastic, and look for the positive side of things. Enthusiasm is something that seems to be contagious. If you are enthusiastic about something, that enthusiasm will spread out to those around you. For instance, when you show enthusiasm in your new efforts to learn how to say No, more than likely, that enthusiasm will spread to those around you, especially those closer to you, resulting in them supporting your efforts even more.

- Try to find the humor in things. When you are a positive individual, it is easier to find the humor in things, making any challenge a lot easier to overcome. Also, put forth an effort to dedicate the energy necessary to overcome hurdles along the way. Lots of energy and looking at things on the bright side will make achieving your goals a lot easier.

- Look at yourself, and act as a problem solver. Very few things in life come easily. There always will be obstacles to overcome and issues to resolve on your way to the finish line. The key is in learning how always to look for a solution to things. When faced with an obstacle, do not think about how impossible it will be to reach your goal because of all these obstacles. Instead, look at them as challenges and learning experiences that will make you stronger. Looking back and seeing how you were able to overcome your obstacles will make you a more positive person because you will see yourself as being able to succeed at anything you set your mind to, rather than a failure at everything because you let obstacles stump you.

- Expect changes, accept them, and embrace them. Think of change as a good thing, not a bad thing. Rather than being afraid of change because it is the unknown, embrace change, and look at it as a new challenge in your life. Accepting the fact that changes happen and that nothing continues the same forever will allow you to accept changes with a positive attitude.

- One of the main keys to having a positive attitude is having the ability to be thankful for what you have. If you spend all your time complaining about all the things that you want and do not have, rather than spending that time contemplating what you actually have and being thankful for it, your attitude will be completely different. When you are able to be grateful for the things that you have, life will seem much better than when you are constantly feeling short-changed. Look hard at all you have and not just the material or tangible things. Rather, look at all those things that make you happy like special friendships, the love of your parents or children, even your spiritual beliefs. Focus on everything that fills you with joy. When you do that, you will realize how much richer you are than what you might think. This exercise alone will give you the biggest boost in attitude than anything else you could do.

You want to learn how to say No because you know that it will be a positive step in your life. You know that having the power to say No effectively will result in your having a more balanced life. Be positive about this challenge you are undertaking, and you will see how easy your road to success will be.

Follow Your Intuition, and Say No

Your intuition is a powerful tool. If more people followed their intuition, they would see how many bad situations they would have been able to avoid. How many times have you proceeded with a decision you have made, knowing it was a bad idea as you were going into it? Probably more often than you care to remember or admit. That was your intuition at work. As accurate as it is for each individual, it is so easy to brush aside and make a decision based on what others think, on what seems like a good idea at the time, or even what you think should be, all the while your inner voice is telling you to do otherwise.

The word "intuition" is rooted in the Latin word *intueri*, which means to comprehend from within your own mind. For centuries, before humanity got so caught up in the scientific approach of things, people made decisions following their intuition. Intuition was thought of as something that belonged back when people were not as "enlightened" by science. Fortunately, humanity seems to be coming around full circle, and intuition is now being recognized as an ability successful people in all walks of life — from spiritual leaders to corporate leaders — use.

In recent years, numerous studies have examined the use of intuition in the corporate world. Daniel Isenberg conducted one of those research studies during his 11-year tenure as faculty at Harvard Business School. As presented in his article published in the *Harvard Business*

Review, "How Senior Managers Think," Isenberg was able to demonstrate that upper management decision makers were making highly effective decisions based on their intuition as much, if not more than, by using logic alone. The report further stated that the higher up the corporate ladder people climbed, the more they rely on their intuition when making decisions.

A Yesaholic confesses: "When I was a senior in high school, I worked part time in a sleep center as a tech, setting up the equipment for that night's patient. I would ensure he or she was comfortable and had everything, and then I would go home. Some nights I would be there for two hours and others, I would be there for up to four hours. Because there was another sleep tech in the office who attended the same high school I did, we always alternated Friday evenings so we both had a chance at having a couple of Friday nights off every month. The night of our high school's last football game for the season (and my last football game as a student), I was scheduled to be off, so I had made plans to attend the game. However, shortly after getting out of school that Friday, I got a call from the sleep center that the other tech had called in sick, and they needed me to come in. I knew he was not sick and that he just wanted to go to the game, but I did not have the courage to tell them that I knew the other tech was not sick. Instead, I told them I could not come in as I had made plans to go to the game. They told me that they understood, but that if I could just come in for only 45 minutes to set up a patient, I could then go. Although I had the feeling that would not be the case, against my better judgment, I agreed. I ended up working for four hours that night, missing the football game, which turned out to be the game that took our team to the state finals. What did I learn from this incident? I learned I should have followed my intuition in that I knew I was going to be there more than the 45 minutes promised and learned to be assertive by telling them that I knew the other tech was not sick. I should have told them he just wanted to go to the football game, and that they should check with him again."

Call it a hunch or a funny feeling, but intuition will alert you of problems and risks to come. How does intuition work? The truth is that no one really knows. Some schools of thought believe it originates from your own subconscious mind. Those who do not believe in intuition call it a wild guess that proved to be right. Regardless of which way you look at it, when you are faced with having to make a decision of saying Yes or No to something that has been asked of you, follow your intuition. Say someone asks something of you, and as you process the information, you intuitively know you are going to say No before you even open your mouth to answer. The reason is that your own subconscious mind has already come up with the resolve that No is the right answer because of a number of reasons that are not evident to you at that instant. At that point, you then follow your intuition and say No, and before you know it, the reasons why you intuitively said No will unfold before your eyes. Maybe not immediately, but sooner than later, it will become clear why you made that decision.

Say No and Feel Good About It: Saying No Without Guilt

The key to being able to say No and not feel guilty about it is to make yourself aware that your plans, desires, and commitments are just as important, if not more, than anyone else's. For example, it is summer, and you and your family have made plans to spend Saturday at the beach. On Friday, your friend calls you and tells you that her husband will be out of town this weekend, so she is coming to your house to visit on Saturday. You tell her that will not be possible because you will not be home Saturday. You should not change your plans to accommodate her when your day of relaxation is just as important as her need for company.

Unless you are able to remove yourself from the old mindsets that everyone should come before you, you will be a slave to everyone else's needs while cheating yourself of what you deserve. If at the moment you are faced with a decision, you are saying, "I really do not have time for this," then you should say No. Your response should be No, so you do not have to compromise what you really want to accommodate the needs of others. Do not feel guilty and say No because there is no guilt on the part of the person asking who may be imposing on your time. Once you have stated your No response, do not dwell on it. Instead, feel good about it. Learn to feel good after you have told someone No, rather than feeling upset and guilty.

Here are some pointers that will help you feel more confident and not feel guilty when you say No. Remember, adapting to this new attitude will not happen overnight, but you will see yourself change a little bit at a time, and the reaction will be automatic rather than something you have to put a great deal of effort into.

Take your time

Before answering any requests for action on your part, take your time to think about what you really want to do. Do not ever feel that you have to be pressured into answering because, more than likely, you will go with the Yes answer, believing it is the path of least resistance. Although some situations will require more consideration than others, every request that entails giving up your time is worthy of consideration. When making major decisions, you need to be able to think about the outcome as long as you see fit. Everyday situations, on the other hand, would not require as much time, but just enough that you feel comfortable with your answer. Once you have determined your answer, you should be guilt-free.

For instance, Monica was a journalist who worked as a staff writer for a women's magazine for several years. Her column in the magazine had a large audience, and the magazine's editor was very pleased with her. Although she worked hard after college to become a staff writer, the constant stress of having to come up with good stories and meet deadlines was starting to take a toll on her. Regardless of the fact that she had a successful career and a bright future ahead of her with this magazine, there came a point in Monica's life where she felt she was at a crossroad, and she had some choices to make. She had been spending all her time saying Yes to all her work responsibilities, even going beyond what was expected of her, but she had been saying No to some family events and even to some time for her to relax. She could continue working for the magazine and continue living the fast-paced life, or she could pursue her dreams of becoming a published author. Leaving a stable job with a good income to pursue a writing career on her own was taking a big leap of faith. But she realized that leaving her current job would allow her to have more time with her family and take care of her own needs.

After taking a couple of weeks to think clearly what she wanted, she took the bold step of saying No to her career as a staff writer for a magazine. Guilt free, she said Yes to a lifestyle that would allow her the time she needed to take care of her needs, reach her goals, and live a less stressful life.

Weigh the pros and cons of the request

Every request deserves a fair evaluation, because if you do not carefully consider the request, then you will feel guilty about your response once it is over and done. Weighing the pros and cons is important because, realistically, you are not always going to be saying No to everything. There will be times when you feel comfortable with the request, and you know that is doable without keeping you from things you want to do, so you will say Yes. However, before that Yes or No comes out of your mouth, it is good to evaluate the benefits or downfalls of a final decision. By doing this, you will be satisfied with your final answer because you know you have evaluated all the possibilities before committing to do something or declining the request.

For instance, Wesley was a young attorney, out of law school for only five years, who had worked at the same law firm for three years. He had plenty of ambition and worked hard; he was hoping to be able to open his own law firm in the future. Because he was relatively new, not only to the field but also the law firm, he did not expect to be asked to be a partner in the firm in the near future. However, shortly after his third year anniversary with the firm, one of the oldest partners retired, and he was asked if he was interested in becoming a partner. Connor, the main partner of the firm, had recommended Wesley as the best candidate due to his work ethic and dedication. Wesley had not foreseen this opportunity, but was extremely excited about it, as he considered the invitation to be a tremendous compliment on his work.

Wesley's initial thought was to say Yes immediately; however, he decided to take time to think about it. There was a lot to consider. If he said Yes to the offer, he would be making a minimum five-year commitment to the firm, based on the contract, plus he would be signing a noncompetitive clause that would not allow him to open his own firm for another five years after the contract was terminated. Saying Yes to this offer would mean saying No to his dreams for at least ten years. He was caught between the opportunity of becoming a partner at an established law firm, which meant security, or following his dreams, which meant taking a chance — a big chance.

After evaluating all the pros and cons, he said No to Connor's offer. As good as it all sounded on the surface, he knew he would be locking himself into a situation that did not allow him to pursue his dreams and did not meet his needs and wants. Shortly thereafter, Wesley left the law firm and went on his own, setting up what later became one of the largest and most prosperous law firms in the city where he lived.

Prepare yourself

Although not applicable in every situation, preparation is an excellent tool to use when you have the opportunity. For instance, when you belong to a social or civic organization, you know about established committees and fundraising activities that are scheduled on a yearly basis. After being a member of such groups for a while, you know the times of the year the organizations will need chairpersons for certain committees or need help on specific tasks. Maybe you were asked in the past to oversee a committee or take care of fundraising activities, and you had agreed to it, which makes you the perfect target to be asked again. In this situation, if you know that you are not going to be able to manage a committee or head a specific fundraising activity, prepare yourself to respond No if you are asked to handle those things again. Preparing yourself to respond in an assertive fashion will prevent you from being caught off guard and being thrust into an unwanted Yes response. Think ahead of time of all the reasons why it would not be a good idea to say Yes. For example, one of your daughters might be getting married in the next six months, and you know you are not going to have any extra time to dedicate to anything other than planning the wedding. In this situation, responding No would be the best answer, and you would not feel guilty about it because you would have given it some thought and knew what was best. In situations where you are asked to do something, and you do not really have reasons other than you do not want to do it, then not wanting to do it is a good reason to say No. When you do not want to do something, you should not force yourself to say Yes because you do not have a tangible reason for it.

Be tactful

When you are tactful and respectful when you say No to somebody, the chances for resistance are drastically diminished, which reduces or avoids the chances of a discussion or confrontation because of the response. By making the process smooth and uneventful, you walk away from the situation with no bad feeling and no regrets, thus no guilt. For example, you are asked to volunteer for cleanup duty after a church event. You do not want to do so, as you have complied numerous times before when asked to help with cleanup. Knowing there are other people who are fully capable of cleaning up but never stay, very tactfully you state that you are not able to say this time, but maybe others who have not participated in the cleanup process can stay. Putting it that way sounds a lot better than saying "I always stay and clean up; ask Jack, Mary, and Sue who always disappear right away and never stay for cleanup duty."

No one likes to feel guilty about things, including saying No to others. However, because of deep-rooted mindsets that you must put others before yourself, along with many other reasons that push people to say Yes when they want to say No, people end up feeling guilty after saying No. Getting over this feeling is just as important and requires as much work as the tendency to say Yes when you want to say No. You may be so used to giving to others that when you start looking out for yourself first, those guilty feelings are quick to overcome you. Nonetheless, you have embarked on a journey of learning how to say No and saying No for all the right reasons. Therefore, learning how not to feel guilty after having said No is a critical part of that journey.

Learning how to say No at the appropriate time and for the appropriate reasons is a lot of work, and it takes commitment as well as a true desire to take on this challenge. You are learning how to say No for your own benefit as well as that of your loved ones. But even though you are learning how to say No, it would be unrealistic to presume that you are going to be saying No to everything. Realistically, there will be occasions when you feel that Yes is the appropriate answer.

CHAPTER ELEVEN

what about those times you must say yes?

WHEN YOU ARE FACED WITH SITUATIONS WHERE YOU have to respond Yes or No to a request, and you want to say Yes; make sure that it what you really want to do. After all that you have learned so far, saying Yes to a major commitment is not the same as saying Yes to everyday tasks you are happy to agree to. Saying No frees you from any commitment, but saying Yes has commitments and consequences tied to it. Before you take that leap and say Yes, make sure that saying Yes is what you really want to do and effectively choose those instances when you feel Yes is the appropriate answer.

Effectively Choosing When To Actually Say Yes

Time is very precious to everyone. It is a resource that will allow you to accomplish your dreams and goals if used wisely. Once time is gone, it cannot be regained; so misused time is wasted time. If you were to think of time as money, and you gave it away to everyone who asked for some of it, you would be poor. You would not even have enough for you to get by. The same holds true with time: If you give your time away to everyone who asked you to do things, then you would not have any time for you or to do the things you wanted.

Before you commit to anything, ask yourself these ten basic questions so you can be sure you know exactly what it is you are agreeing to:

1. Do I really want to agree to do what I have been asked to do?

2. How much of my time will I have to invest in this?

3. Am I going to benefit from this experience?

4. What will my role be and what is the extent of my responsibility?

5. Is it possible that I will have the opportunity to do this again?

6. What am I not going to be able to do if I say Yes to this?

7. If I need help with this task, is help going to be available?

8. Is this a cause/project I believe in?

9. Is this going to help me reach my goals or take time away from my efforts to reach my goals?

10. Am I being asked because I am the right person, or am I being asked because I usually say Yes?

Before you agree to anything, make sure it is something you will enjoy or, at least, not dread. Agreeing to do something and then realizing in the middle of the task you have no interest in continuing is bad news. That is why it is critical that you are 100 percent sure of what you want before you accept. Also, evaluate how much time completing this task will take away from other things that you want to do. Although it may be something that could possibly fall within the list of things you want to do, you need to be conscious of how much time it will take away from your other commitments. Because, even though you may want to do it, time-wise it may be prohibitive for you to accept.

Although you might want to do something and are ready to say Yes to the request, you must take a moment to evaluate whether you will benefit from the experience. Consider whether the commitment is going to provide you with experience and knowledge that will benefit you in the future in any possible way. If you are going to invest your time and effort in any one task, you should really make the best of it and gain the most out of it so that it will not be wasted time. Think about what role will you play and the extent of your responsibility. Sometimes you may agree to do something that will only take a few minutes of your time and very little effort. There is a big difference between agreeing to help with something and actually being in charge of the event. Having a clear understanding about what is being asked from the beginning can make a difference between whether you accept or decline. You might have a couple of hours to set up the tables for the fundraiser, but you may not have a whole day to be in charge of the entire setup for the event.

There are instances where you are asked to do something, and you tend to jump right into it because you think this is a "once in a lifetime opportunity," when, in actuality, it is something that you can take on at a later date. Before making a commitment to something, maybe at a time when you really do not have a lot of spare time, find out if the opportunity will be available to you again in the future.

Say you have always wanted to chair the parent teacher association for your children's school, and although you have held different positions in the association, the opportunity to actually chair the association had never presented itself. However, this school year you were asked if you wanted to chair the school's PTA, and as much as you want to do it, you realize that you have a new job that requires you to travel a lot. Taking the position of chair would be accomplishing something you always wanted, but this is really not the best time. You will not be able to dedicate as much time to this endeavor as needed to do a good job. So, as much as you would like to help and say Yes, you respond with a No because you know you do not have the available time this commitment will require.

When you consider accepting a request for something you know requires more than your talents and efforts alone to complete effectively, you must consider whether help will be available to you. You may be asked to do something that you really wish to do, but if help is not going to be available, you may consider not accepting at all. Your goal should always be that when you accept to do something, you should always do it right or not at all. If your ability to complete the task effectively is going to be compromised by the lack of help, you should postpone taking on the task until a later date when help might be available.

Believing in what you do is an essential element to succeeding at what you are doing. Agreeing to do something because you have the extra time or because it will look good on your résumé should not be good enough reasons to accept any request. If you do not believe in the cause, the project, or even the people asking, then do not agree to it regardless of how inclined you might be to do so. You might just find yourself in a situation where conflicts of interests may arise, making your ability to complete what was asked of you almost impossible.

For instance, say your neighbor is collecting signatures to present a complaint to the homeowners association about people parking their work vehicles, with business signs all over them, in front of their houses. Not only does he want you to sign the petition, but also he wants you to help him pass the petition around to other neighbors. But you do not agree with the petition because you think it is perfectly OK for people to park their cars, regardless of whether they are work vehicles, in front of their property. As much as you like your neighbor and wish you could help, you do not believe in this cause and collecting signatures for it will be a conflict of interest. It will be impossible for you to represent something you do not believe in, so you turn his request down.

Along the same lines, you must consider whether the undertaking you are considering accepting is something that will help you reach your goals in life. Whether it is a career-oriented goal or a personal life enrichment goal, if the answer is No, reconsider whether you still want to say Yes.

Think about your skills and talents and what you may be able to bring to the table should you agree to do what was asked of you. If you believe you fall short of what is required to tackle the matter at hand, then you should wonder if you were asked because you were the right person for the job, or you were asked because you always say Yes. Should the latter be the case, do not agree to do anything knowing that you were asked because you normally would say Yes. Take pride in who you are. You are not anybody's "Yes" person; you are a very special individual who should be valued for who you are. If you were not asked because of your talents or strengths, then redirect your talents and abilities into other efforts that will be more appreciated.

For instance, say your daughter attends a small private school where you are always very active, always volunteering and taking on whatever needs to be accomplished. One day you are asked to coach the girls' junior varsity basketball team because the girls would like to have a team, but the school does not have a coach. Having never coached or even played basketball, you know you are being asked to take on a responsibility probably because you always say Yes to every request, not because of your abilities. You realize this commitment will require a large amount of time, as you will have to attend several games and practices for several months. You also realize that not only will you not be providing the girls with a fair chance at winning, but you also would be taking valuable time away from other things that really need your attention. As a result, you end up saying No and suggesting they contact another parent who may be better qualified.

Negotiating a Yes

If you are considering agreeing to something that has been asked of you, you have looked at all the factors surrounding this task, and you are convinced that accepting is not going to infringe on your personal time or any plans you might have already made — but only if the commitment can be adjusted a little bit. You can partially say Yes because in order for you to accept the task, some of the terms of the commitment will have to be adjusted to fit your schedule. You are willing to accept but some give and take will have to take place; you are going to have to negotiate the terms of the request.

Vanessa was a customer service representative at a bank for two years, and the branch manager approached her and offered her the assistant branch manager's position, which had recently become vacant. This was a great opportunity for Vanessa, and she was seriously considering accepting it. She took into consideration what the job would entail, pay, benefits, and what skills and experience she would need to accomplish her job effectively. She knew she had the experience and skills necessary to accomplish this task because prior to joining the current bank, she was assistant branch manager for five years at another bank. However, before she accepted, some of the terms of the proposed promotion would have to be negotiated. For instance, the pay had to be negotiated, as there was no proposed pay increase. Also, the proposed schedule would have to be negotiated as she would be expected to work every Saturday morning rather than alternating with someone else. In addition, she was not being afforded any additional benefits that were normally part of the package for the management team. Vanessa met with the branch manager, and after being able to successfully negotiate the terms of the promotion, Vanessa accepted the offer.

When you are negotiating a Yes, prior to negotiating, you need to know your bottom line. If you do not know what that bottom line is, then how would you know if you have been successful in your negotiation? In any negotiation, there is plenty of give and take, so you have to be prepared to know how much you are willing to give, and how much you will take. If, at the end of the day, you feel that you gave in more than you really wanted to, then you are not going to be happy with your decision, which makes that Yes answer the wrong answer. It then becomes one of those situations where you should have said No instead.

Monique and Eric have been dating for several years, and every year for Super Bowl, Eric goes to his friend's house for a Super Bowl party. However, this year Eric decided he wanted to have the party at his house, and without telling Monique, he made plans with his friends to have the party at his house. The day before the game, Eric gave Monique a list of supplies for the party that he would like for her to pick up when she went to the grocery store. Infuriated at the fact that Eric had planned a party at their house without consulting her, Monique refused to get the groceries and told Eric to get them himself. As they proceeded to discuss the party, Eric's contention was that he could not cancel it now because everyone had made plans to come and would have nowhere else to go. He apologized and pleaded with her to agree to have the party at their house. After some discussion, Monique agreed to the party and the grocery shopping, but her bottom line was she was not going to have a thing to do with it other than the shopping. Eric would have to prepare the snacks, take care of his guests for the day, and clean up afterward. Although Monique was not happy with the event, she agreed to it under her terms and set the bottom line as to how much she would actually participate on the event, which was just the shopping.

When considering whether to negotiate a Yes from a request that you were initially considering saying No to, you must first determine whether the request can be negotiated. The following criteria will help you identify such requests:

- Is the request something that really interests you?
- Is there enough "wiggle" room within the terms of the request to make adjustments that meet your schedule?
- Will accomplishing the task under your terms still have the same desired outcome?

Ultimately, the most fundamental element to negotiating a Yes answer is that at the end you are satisfied with the terms and outcome of the request. Sometimes you want to say Yes because you agree with the concept of the request, and you want to be of assistance the best you can, which is the key to a positive outcome — complying the best you can. If you are going to agree to something, remember it has to be something that will not conflict with your interests or take time away from those things that are important to you. This is the whole idea behind learning how to say No: to keep you from making commitments that are beyond your means and committing for all the wrong reasons. In the end, you end up frustrated at yourself and even those around you because your needs did not get met.

Living With The Choice You Made And Learning From It

Only you can decide whether the correct answer in any given situation should be Yes or No. You have been provided with the tools to make the decision that will better serve you. However, that is not to say that there may still be times when you make the wrong decision. You have to deal with the consequences that arise. When you make the wrong decision, and there are bad consequences to deal with, try to maintain a positive outlook on things. Think about what you might have learned from the experience, and take it as an opportunity for growth.

For instance, Janice was asked if she wanted to volunteer as a foster caregiver for a pet rescue group in her community. She considered all the pros and cons and could not find any downfalls in agreeing to participate. Although she agreed knowing that there would not be any financial reward for her efforts, there would be many heartfelt nonfinancial rewards. The time she would invest would be mostly in the form of giving love and attention, both of which she had a lot to give, to abandoned small pets. What Janice did not know at the time she accepted is that her financial commitment to the effort was going to be more than expected. She knew she would be responsible for supplying the feed for her foster pets, which she assumed could not be much if the pets were small. However, after only being part of the rescue effort for a short while, she started to get assigned to larger breed dogs, which ate two or three times more than the smaller breeds. Her good will and heartfelt intentions soon were overcome by stress and anxiety as it was becoming increasingly difficult for her to feed these pets on her very modest income. In this case, what seemed to have been the right decision at the time had unforeseen consequences and the conviction that she would never do something like that again. Unfortunately, bad decisions are the types of experiences that teach you a lesson and hopefully keep you from making worse mistakes in the future.

On the other side of the coin, hopefully there will be many more times when you will make the right decision, and you will receive a direct benefit from such choice. You have the choice of making the most out of the benefits reaped and putting them to work for you in future decisions you make, or you can just enjoy the immediate gratification and put any lessons learned aside. The route those who excel in life take is that of taking the lessons learned and using them as springboards to forge ahead. When you chose to put what you have learned into play and use that information as you encounter other decision-making opportunities, your decision-making skills will improve, allowing you to make even more of the right decisions.

For example, Daniel was new in the business of buying and selling thoroughbreds. On one occasion while at a training racetrack, he was approached by Stan, who had been in the business of buying and selling racehorses for a long time. Stan offered Daniel a great deal on a 2-year-old colt born to a mare that had many wins on the track. The deal seemed too good to be true as both the mare and the stud had excellent bloodlines, making this colt worth even more. The offer was pretty much too hard to resist; however, following his gut feeling, Daniel asked Stan to give him some time to think about it and get back to him. Stan insisted on making the deal that day, further stating that he had other buyers interested, and the one who came forward with the money first would take the colt. He insisted

> *that Daniel would be missing out on a great opportunity if he did not buy it. Still, Daniel asked for some time to think the offer over. After a few days of thinking the issue over, Daniel contacted Stan and told him he was not interested, and Stan responded that it did not matter because he had already sold the colt. As it turned out, Daniel had made the right decision in declining to purchase the colt because the colt happened to have problems with one of his legs that was not detected until later when it was too late to back out of the sale. This is truly a situation where having said No regardless of the insistence of others was the right decision. Daniel could have lost his money and, instead, was able to use that money to make a better investment later on.*

Learning how to say No is a learned skill that takes assertiveness and self-empowerment to accomplish. Take appropriate steps to ensure you say Yes during the instances when you actually want to do so. Whatever decision you make, be 100 percent sure that taking that step is what you wanted and intended it to be. More often than not, once you have taken the leap and either committed or declined to do something, there is no going back. After you have said Yes to something, going back on your word will make you look bad and let some people down. When you say No to something because you are convinced that is not what you want, there should be no going back either. When you say No to something, it is because you mean it, and you should stick to your answer.

CHAPTER TWELVE

when no means no

HOW MANY TIMES HAVE YOU ANSWERED SOMEONE'S request with a No, only to have a counter answer of "I can't believe you just said No" or "What do you mean, No?" somehow expecting you to change your mind? Unfortunately, you probably will hear those statements even more now that you are using your No responses more frequently and with more assertiveness. But with your new set of skills on how to be more assertive, it should not be a problem for you to reaffirm that No is your response. Do not let yourself get intimidated by such comments as "I do not take No for an answer" because it is not the person asking the question who has a choice whether to say Yes or No. You are the one making the choice, and you can always say No any time you see fit. Remember, you have the final say in the choices you make.

Say No and Stick to It

Learning to stick to your No answer is just as important, if not more, than having answered with a No. After all, what good is it to say No only to later take it back? You have placed a great deal of time and effort in learning how to say No, and you do not want to have it wasted by not being able to stick to your decision. Standing behind your No answer may not be the easiest thing to do at first, but with enough self-discipline and determination, it can be done.

One of the most common situations where people tend to waver is when it comes to their kids. After listening to enough nagging and whining, often parents get tired of listening to it and just give in. This is a mistake, because once you give in to their begging, they will try the same technique again because it works. When you answer them, make sure No is what you want to say before you say it, thereby avoiding having to go back on your word later. Think about the consequences of giving in to a request (after much begging) to which you initially said No because you knew accepting would only add chaos to your life. The outcome was probably as you expected: added chaos.

Abby has two children ages 10 and 11. Since visiting their cousins who just got a new puppy, they have been begging Abby for a puppy. For days Abby continued to tell them No because taking care of a dog required a great deal of time, which she did not have. Because of her children's age, she knew she could not count on them to take care of the new pet. After growing tired of listening to them beg and whine for days, she was ready to put a stop to the nonsense. Instead of giving in, as she normally would have before she learned to say No, she found a way to put an end to the struggle. She went to the public library and checked out a book on taking care of new puppies, brought it home, sat the children down, and showed them all it would entail to take care of the new pet, so they could fully understand the extent of what their responsibilities would be. She further stated that she knew that at this time they were not ready for a pet, and that it was best to wait a while longer before they considered adopting a pet. Being old enough to understand, they agreed to wait and get the puppy later.

Another prime example of situations where standing firm behind your No answer is important is at work. It is easy for people to fall into a pattern of saying Yes at the workplace because they tend to think their job would be on the line if they answered otherwise. When you say No at work, say to the coworker who is always dumping extra work on you, you should not even consider taking back that No because you know that saying Yes will result in your work doubling. When your workload doubles, you end up working late, stressing over all the things that you need to do but cannot get to, and ultimately feeling overwhelmed. Your work also suffers because you cannot dedicate the time it deserves. All of these instances are the very reasons why you are learning to say No. Any time you have the slightest inkling of taking back a No, think about all of the above and you will see how quickly that urge disappears.

How about saying No and sticking to it when it comes to everyday requests?

> *For example, you are having dinner, and your friend calls. You answer the phone, and she asks you if you have a minute because she had something to run by you. However, you know that when that friend calls, the calls are never brief, regardless of what they may be about. You tell her that you do not have a minute now because you are having dinner and will call her back when you are done. Still, she insists that she only needs a minute and starts her story. At that point, you then interrupt her and tell her that you cannot talk to her at the moment and will call her back when you are done so that you can give her your undivided attention. You then say, "Talk to you soon, OK?" wait for her to say "OK," and then hang up. You do call her back when you are done with dinner, thereby keeping your word.*

Whether you are saying No to a simple request or a major undertaking, being confident and assertive enough to stand behind your answer will be essential to your success. Always think back to the reasons why you said No in the first place, and more than likely, that would be enough to keep you strong on your decision.

When a No Results in Confrontation

Every situation you encounter is different, and even when two situations are quite similar, the outcome of each of these, more than likely, will be different. For that very reason, it will be unrealistic to assume that every time you encounter "X" situation, your response should be "this," and the result will be "that." There may be situations where you are asked to do something, and your No response unexpectedly results in an intense reaction from another person that leads to a confrontation. Having the necessary skills and tools available so you can effectively react to the situation will prevent the situation from escalating any further.

You own an automobile mechanic shop and just completed repair work on a customer's vehicle. When the customer picks up his car, he complains that there is a scratch on the passenger's side door and demands that you have it repaired. You proceed to explain to him that the scratch was already there when he brought the car in, and that you will not repair the scratch. Hearing your response, the customer starts yelling, insulting you, and demanding that you take responsibility for the scratch and repair it. Once you realize the situation is getting out of hand, rather than engaging in a confrontation, you take a deep breath to calm your nerves. With an even tone of voice, you let your customer know that you understand his frustration and further explain how the scratch did not

> *occur there. Throughout the conversation, you always keep your emotions under control until you both reach an amicable solution.*

When saying No to something escalates into a confrontation, taking the following steps will help ease the tension and hopefully lead into an amicable resolution for all parties involved.

Take a deep breath

When you take a deep breath, you are clearing all the negativity and are opening yourself up to understanding and clear communication, thereby allowing yourself time to analyze what your response to the request should be.

Relax

Relaxing will allow you to communicate your side of the story better, as well as allow you to understand better what the other party is trying to communicate to you.

Use an even tone of voice

Maintaining an even, clear, and friendly tone of voice is always helpful when soothing the other person's temper.

Listen

Listen to what the other party has to say and acknowledge his or her comments. Although you have made up your mind when you said No and are fully prepared to stand behind your answer, listen to what they have to say. It will make them feel better and maybe give you a clearer understanding as to why a simple No answer generated such a confrontation.

Keep your emotions under control

Do not engage in a confrontational discussion. Keep your emotions under control if you want to keep the confrontation to a minimum and salvage the relationship, whether is personal or professional.

Acknowledge the other party's emotions

Acknowledge that you understand he or she is upset about your having said No, as this will show respect for that other person.

Clarify your intentions

Make it clear to the other party that it was never your intention to upset him or her with your answer. Let the other party know that as important as it was for him or her that you answered Yes, it was just as important to you to have answered No. Tell him or her you had valid reasons for saying No, and that you wish he or she would respect that.

Find a common ground

Try to find a common ground to the situation — points of view you both share. Maybe both parties can understand where each other comes from in respect to what was expected and what was received in return.

Moving forward

Reiterate to the other party how important the relationship is to you (if applicable) and ask how you can work together to move forward from that moment.

Any resistance that turns into confrontation as a result of having said No to somebody can occur when people who are used to your saying Yes all the time are faced with reoccurring No's coming from you. All the people who have benefited from your constant Yeses are accustomed to you always taking care of things. Hearing a No may come as a surprise to some people. If the request is for something in the near future, even though it may be frustrating for the person asking and could cause some hard feelings, after you say No there may still be time to find an alternative solution.

What happens when the request is for something that requires immediate action, and you were asked under the assumption you would say Yes? In such a case, being able to find a substitute on short notice might be nearly impossible, which will definitely cause distress in the party asking. Either way, it is not your fault that the person asking assumed you would take care of the situation and was not prepared to find someone else to take care of the matter. The best you can do in situations such as this is try to ease the tension and work through the situation to a peaceful resolution.

A confrontation might also arise in situations where the person asking something of you may be asking you as a last resort and may actually be under great stress. You might seem like the best option for releasing their frustration because you just said No to something that might have solved their problems. Keeping this in mind will help you cope with the possible outburst you may encounter in such situations and allow you to step out of the confrontational atmosphere a little quicker.

For instance, your boss is under pressure from his boss to complete a project by a certain date. The due date is rapidly approaching, and the project is nowhere near completed. Your boss starts to stress and out of desperation and frustration asks you to complete a portion of the project, which you are not qualified to do. You know you are not qualified to take on this task, but you also know that because of his state of mind, he is going to become agitated when you tell him you cannot comply. Being mindful of this, when the outburst takes place, instead of being defensive and adding fuel to the fire, stating that you will see what you can do will ease the tension. Once he has calmed down, you can then approach him with possible solutions to his dilemma.

Propose An Alternative

Proposing an alternative to what is being asked of you not only eases the jolt of having said No, but it also keeps the doors open for a positive relationship between the two parties. The alternative proposed may not be exactly what the person who asked wanted, but if it is close enough, it will work for both parties involved. The problem with a No answer is that it frequently frustrates the person who asked because it makes him/her feel powerless. You should counteract the situation by offering an alternative (or alternatives) that then allows the person who asked to feel empowered once again.

For example, Kyle, one of your team members at work, asks you if you could take care of his speaking engagement in San Francisco at the end of the week because his assistant inadvertently scheduled him for two functions at the same time. You are not able to take his place because you have a meeting with a customer out of town that same day. So you tell him that you cannot take care of his speaking engagement because of other commitments, but that you are aware that Sally, one of the other team members, does not have anything scheduled then and maybe she can take care of it for him. Although you just told him No, you also just gave him a possible solution to his dilemma.

Here are some examples of situations where you can say No to the request but still provide the person who asked with an alternative solution that will more than likely take care of the request.

- *Your out-of-town friend calls you and tells you that he is coming to visit for a couple of days, and he is bringing his yellow Labrador retriever, Diesel, with him. You do not allow large dogs in your house, so you tell him that you do not have a problem with him coming to visit, but you hope he does not mind you making arrangements with the nearby dog kennel so that Diesel can stay there during his stay at your house.*

- *Your friend from high school who is in the Army calls you and asks if it would be possible for you to pick her up at the airport Thanksgiving morning because she wants to surprise her parents. The airport is an hour away and going to pick her up will conflict with your Thanksgiving plans because you are having Thanksgiving at two different households. So, you tell her that you cannot pick her up because of commitments with family but you will be glad to suggest a couple of mutual friends whom you know do not have plans until late that evening.*

- *During summer vacation, your uncle asks you to house-sit for him over the weekend while he goes on a hunting trip out of state. You tell him that you cannot house-sit for him because you have already made plans to go camping with friends. However, you suggest he check with your sister who is always looking for ways to stay busy during summer vacation.*

If you propose an alternative solution when you say No, it shows that you have given the request some thought rather than discarding it as unimportant. The show of good will and care always goes a long way in softening a No response.

Practice Makes Perfect

Saying No does not come easily to most people, which is why you must actually teach yourself to say No. You must practice saying No so that saying No will flow naturally. Here are some pointers on how to go about it:

- A good way to start is by saying No to simple things, such as your kids begging for ice cream after school.

- Try saying No at least several times a week to things you would normally say Yes to, such as telemarketers' phone calls. Do not listen to the whole thing if you are not interested in what they are selling or their cause; just say "No. I am not interested. Thank you." And hang up.

- As you are driving or alone at home, present yourself with possible scenarios of situations where you normally have a hard time saying No, but normally end up saying Yes. These instances can include situations such as taking care of the neighbor's dogs when they are out of town, although they never offer or seem to be available to take care of your pets when you need them. Practice saying No to the request. Hear yourself saying it and experience the feeling of having said No.

- Practice in the mirror saying No if you feel that seeing yourself saying No will give you more strength.

- As you learn and get used to saying No more often, take a deep cleansing breath before answering any request. This will not only give you second to compose yourself but also will also help build your courage to answer accordingly.

If you are more of a visual person, then you should develop a chart where you can record your progress each week as to how many times you said Yes and how many times you said No. In the first column, list the request. Then have a Yes column and a No column where the answer you provide to that request. The last column should be the "Did I feel good about it?" column where you will say Yes or No. It will give you an excellent overview of what things you have been able to move from normally saying Yes to now saying No. It will also serve you as a reminder of those things that you said Yes to but did not feel good about it later, which will help you to avoid saying Yes to such requests in the future. *A sample of this chart is available in Appendix A — Saying No Progress Record.*

The Feeling of Freedom When You Learn to Say No

You know the feeling you experience when you are able to lift a heavy burden off your shoulders? What about that overpowering feeling you get when you achieve a goal that seemed almost impossible to attain? Well, that is the feeling you experience when you finally learn how to say a firm and assertive No. Once kind of No has come out of your mouth, you know you have driven the message home, and you are completely OK with it.

When you empower yourself and become more assertive, projecting a loud and clear No with conviction as if it is second nature, that is when you know you have arrived. It is the exhilarating feeling you get from knowing that you are no longer anybody's first person to visit when they need an easy Yes response. You know you are free from the burden that too many Yeses can cause when you are able to spend more time doing the things you enjoy. You know you have succeeded when you are able to think of your needs and wants before you agree to anything that may jeopardize your ability to have those needs and wants met.

Learning how to say No gives you the freedom and self-confidence to say No to your boss when he or she makes unrealistic demands, No to nagging and whining children, and No to the constant requests for favors that keep you scrambling to get things done. Take a moment to think about how you felt when all you were doing was pleasing others, taking care of everyone's needs but your own, and not having any time to yourself because you were busy tending to others. Looking back, you probably realize how stressed and overwhelmed you felt. Now, think about all the possibilities your newfound freedom has in store for you.

Learning how to say No can open up a whole new world of opportunities for you. You are no longer unable to accept new challenges because you are too busy taking care of everybody else's challenges. In the process of learning how to say No, you learned how to empower yourself and become more assertive, which allowed you to become a confident individual. You have become an individual who is now ready to take on new challenges and opportunities that might have not come up unless you had said No at the right time.

SO, YOU WANTED TO LEARN HOW TO SAY NO. YOU took the initiative of looking for assistance on how to break the horrible habit of usually saying Yes when you really wanted to say No. You are to be commended for taking such a step toward liberating yourself from your own inability to say No. So many people go their entire lives saying Yes to everything and then regret it later. Not only do all those who always want something of them control their lives, but they also live their lives making sacrifices trying to keep everyone happy but themselves.

People's habit of saying Yes all the time is something that is deeply rooted within them as a result of their upbringing, their need to be liked and accepted, and even because they just feel they have to say Yes. Regardless of what the reasons might have been as to why you were always saying Yes, you are now ready to work through those issues and move forward ready to say No when you would have otherwise said Yes.

Becoming a more assertive and confident person is the backbone of your ability to effectively say No with conviction when you feel the need to do so. Giving yourself the credit and self-worth you deserve is important so that you can value yourself and place great importance in having your needs met. When you are constantly saying Yes to others, you are putting their needs and wants first, thereby sabotaging yourself. When this happens, you start to suffer physically and mentally from all the stress and exhaustion resulting from your constantly going without giving yourself a chance to catch up.

Remember that it is OK to say No to friends, at work, and even to your family. You do not need to give them all kinds of reasons and excuses as to why you said No; you say No when you feel No is the right answer. If you are not sure, keep in mind these questions that will help you make a decision.

- Do I really want to do this?
- Do I have time for this?
- How much time will it take to accomplish this task?
- What is really going to happen if I say No?
- Is there someone else, in the family or at work, who can take care of this rather than me?
- Does it fit within my priorities?
- Am I giving up something I really wanted to do for myself to take care of this?

Do not forget that every time you say Yes to something that someone wants you to take care of, you are saying No to another task. This other task may be something you are keenly interested in and could dedicate some time to, or even something you wanted to do for yourself.

Empower yourself with confidence, and make it one of your main goals to live a balanced life of Yeses and No's. Having learned how to say No does not mean that you will not allow yourself to say Yes to anything unless it will directly benefit you, because that is not the case. You will always be there for your family and friends as they will always be there for you, but all within reason. Your children and your spouse will still love you, as well as your parents, siblings, and extended family, when you start saying No to them. They may not like it at first, but, eventually, they will get used to your new outlook and accept you for who you are and who you have become. The only difference between when you used to always say Yes and now that you have learned to say No is that now you have learned to establish some boundaries and can now have a healthy relationship with all those around you.

During this journey of learning the art of saying No, you have learned whom you can say No to, the reasons why you should say No more often, and you have learned that it is OK to say No freely and without guilt. You also have learned different ways in which you can say No, even to the most persuasive people, and how to handle difficult situations while still being able to say No effectively. All this entails change in how you have been operating and doing things for a long time, and as such, you must keep it ever so present to be patient with yourself, as change takes time. Your change into the new assertive you, a you capable of holding your own and saying No when you should, will take time but will be worth the time you invest. Any change that will be lasting will take time to put into practice and adapt to. Therefore, remember to seek support if you want to succeed. Whether it is support from your loved ones or from support groups, seeking the support of those around will help make your journey through this great change in your life much easier.

Learning how to say No is not just about learning how get the word to come out of your mouth at the right time, it is also about you having a positive attitude that will make it happen. A positive attitude in anything you set yourself to do in this life will help make success a reality. The word No is a very powerful word. Mastering using the word No will help you reduce your stress level and will allow you more free time so that you can enjoy life more. You will certainly like the person you have become better than the person you used to be. Seeing yourself as an assertive, secure individual will not only give you the ability to say No, but also will give you the wings you need to enjoy some new challenges and opportunities.

"The art of leadership is saying No, not Yes.
It is very easy to say Yes." — TONY BLAIR

learning how to say no progress record

Progress Record

	Request	Yes/No	Did I feel good about it?
Week #			
Week #			

	Request	Yes/No	Did I feel good about it?
Week #			
Week #			
Week #			

quick reference guide to saying no

DURING THIS PROCESS OF LEARNING HOW TO SAY NO, you have been exposed to numerous situations where a request is made and possible No responses have been provided to such situations. You also have learned the tools that you need to make your decision based on what is best for you. The information is extensive and the scenarios, tools, and skills to learn are spread throughout the book in various sections, which is why this Appendix will serve you as a quick reference guide. This chapter offers information that is easy to access when you feel you need a refresher on how to say No and some quick No responses to common requests.

How to Say No, in a Nutshell

The following is a summary of the steps discussed at length in this book on how to say No and how to implement what you have learned. Here is a quick reference point where you can refresh your mind of the key points of what you have learned.

1. Think about why is it that you always find yourself saying Yes.
    a. Is it because of what you were taught as a child?
    b. Is it because you want to be liked?
    c. Is it because you feel that "you have to" say Yes?
    d. Is it because you are not assertive enough and do not have the courage to just say No?

2. Establish and accept that you should be the No. 1 priority in your life.
    a. Having your needs met is as important, if not more, than meeting the needs of others.
    b. Not having your needs met can result in physical and mental distress.

3. Understand that No is a complete sentence, and there are no excuses needed.

4. When you say No, you must be firm and state your No with conviction.

5. It is OK to say No to friends, family, and at work.

6. Think about your actions in the past, and come to terms with yourself as to why you really said Yes. Was it because:
    a. You felt that if you did not say Yes, nobody else would?

b. You felt that no one could accomplish a specific task as well as you could?

c. You felt like being the martyr?

d. You wanted to say Yes just to be able to say you did it?

7. You must live a balanced lifestyle of Yeses and No's, which means:

   a. You must motivate yourself to change from always saying Yes to saying No.

   b. You must empower yourself to be able to make that change.

8. There is nothing wrong with seeking the support of others as you make your transition from usually saying Yes to No.

   a. Seek support from friends and family.

   b. Join more structured support groups available in your community through churches and other organizations.

   c. Join online forums on the subject.

9. You must learn to be assertive.

   a. Learn to effectively communicate your needs, desires, and feelings.

   b. Do not be afraid to say No.

   c. Always communicate with confidence, using body language that projects assertiveness.

10. It is all about attitude. Have a positive attitude in life and be able to change from usually saying Yes to learning how to say No.
    a. Establish attainable goals so that you can experience success.
    b. Start fresh every day, and take one day at a time.
    c. Do not let fear of the unknown stop you.

11. Say No, and do not feel guilty about your decision.
    a. Keep in mind that your plans, desires, and commitments are just as important, if not more, than anyone else's.

12. Be choosy about to whom you say Yes.
    a. Decide whether you really want to do what is asked of you.
    b. Think about whether you believe in this cause/project.
    c. Is this undertaking going to help you reach your goals?

13. Say No and stick to it. When you say No, you mean No.
    a. Be confident and assertive enough to stand behind your answer.

14. Remember, practice always makes perfect. Practice saying No.
    a. Start by saying No to simple requests.
    b. Practice when you are alone, saying No to possible scenarios.

Quick No Answers to Keep Handy

Every day you get bombarded with requests, all of which expect you to say Yes. Having spent time and effort in learning how to say No, you should be an expert by now in coming up with quick No responses to those everyday, common requests. However, as you get better in the art of saying No, here is a quick reference guide to help you with saying No to the most common questions to which you normally would have said Yes.

You get a call. "Hi, I am conducting a telephone survey about 'X' service. It will only take a few minutes."	*"No, I do not have a few minutes. I would appreciate you not calling again."*
"Dinner was excellent. How about if we split the check?"	*"No, your meals were more than ours. You take care of your check, and I will take care of mine."*
"I am involved with a new program where I can make money from home. The more people you sign up, the more money you make. Do you want to come over tonight, and I will tell you all about it?"	*"No, thank you. I do not get involved with pyramid income arrangements."*
"Can you loan me some money?"	*"No, I cannot. I have a policy not to lend anybody money."*

You get a call. "Hi, I am with the 'X' foundation, and I was hoping you could make a donation to our cause."	"I appreciate your efforts, but I do not take telephone solicitations. Please do not call here again."
You get a call, "Hi, I am with your cable (or telephone company), and I want to take a few minutes of your time to go over your current service packet."	"Thank you, but I like the service as is. I will call you if I want any changes."
"Can I bring a couple of friends with me to the party?"	"No, I cannot accommodate anybody else."
"Can I borrow your car?"	"No, I do not lend my car to anybody."
"I know you only came to get your hair cut today, but how about if we color it a new shade as well?"	"No, thank you. I just need it cut."
"Can you fudge the information on the form so that I can qualify for financial assistance?"	"No, I cannot do that. That would not only be unethical, but also illegal."
"Can you cover my shift for me this weekend? I really want to go to the beach with my friends."	"No, I cannot. I already made plans to go to the beach myself."

"Can you stay late (at work) again today?"	*"No. I cannot. I have plans with my family right after work."*
"Can I come crash at your place tonight?"	*"No, I do not have the extra space."*
"Can you pick me up and give me a ride again today?"	*"No. I cannot. I have given you a ride every day this week, and today I will not be able to bring you back."*
"Can you help me again with this project as you always have?"	*"No, I cannot. Maybe it is time you have someone else take care of it."*
"I am running late; can you wait for me?"	*"No. You are always late, and I am not going to be late again because of you."*
"You are coming to my house again for the holidays this year?"	*"No, this year we are staying home."*
"Can you take care of my dogs while I am out of town?"	*"Not this time. I have made other plans."*

Your massage therapist (or other service professional) tells you, "While you are here, let us go ahead and schedule your next five visits."	*"No, thank you. I will call you and schedule my next appointment when I am ready for another massage (service)."*
"I know you have a lot of work to do already, but can you train the new employee for me in the morning?"	*"No, I cannot. I have a deadline to meet and I do not have the extra time."*
You get a call while having dinner and the person says, "Do you have a minute so I can talk to you?"	*"No, I am having dinner. I will call you when I am done."*
"I hate filling out forms. Can you fill this out for me, and I will just sign it?"	*"No, I hate filling out forms just as much as you do. You can fill it out. I did mine."*
When someone makes an offensive comment to you, your response should be:	*"That comment was out of line, and I would appreciate it if you did not say that again."*

BIBLIOGRAPHY

Breitman, Patty and Connie Hatch. *How to Say No Without Feeling Guilty*. New York: Broadway Books, 2000.

Dale, Paulette. *Did You Say Something, Susan? How Any Woman Can Gain Confidence With Assertive Communication*. Secaucus, New Jersey: Carol Publishing, 1999.

Isenberg, Daniel J. "How Senior Managers Think," *Harvard Business Review*, November-December 1984. Accessed March 21, 2011. **www.drjudithorloff.com/Free-Articles/How-Senior-Managers-Think.pdf**.

"Maslow's Hierarchy." Changing Minds.org. Accessed March 21, 2011. **www.changingminds.org/explanations/needs/maslow.htm**

McCoy, Charles W. Jr.. *Why Didn't I Think of That?* Paramus, New Jersey: Prentice Hall Press, 2002.

Newman, Susan. *The Book of No: 250 Ways to Say It — And Mean It and Stop People-Pleasing Forever*. New York: McGraw-Hill, 2005.

Paterson, Randy J. *The Assertiveness Workbook*. Oakland, California: New Harbinger Publications, Inc., 2000.

Stalter, Harmony. *Employee Body Language Revealed: How to Predict Behavior in the Workplace by Reading and Understanding Body Language*. Ocala, Florida: Atlantic Publishing Group, Inc., 2010.

"The Seed of Apple's Innovation." *Bloomberg Businessweek* October 12, 2004. Accessed March 21, 2011. **www.businessweek.com/bwdaily/dnflash/oct2004/ nf20041012_4018_db083.htm.**

Ury, William. *The Power Of A Positive No: How to Say No and Still Get to Yes*. New York: Bantam Books, 2008.

 Born in Michigan to Cuban parents, Maritza has been able to experience a rich and well-rounded life, being able to enjoy both the American culture and the Cuban culture. Maritza started working with the local government at the age of 16 and continued working there through college and beyond. During her employment, she moved up through the ranks from part-time secretary to becoming the Foreign Trade Zone manager. With more than 25 years of experience in the business sector, both private and public, Maritza is able to provide practical insight into the many situations in which one must learn to say No when you would otherwise say Yes. She is able to provide insight from the boss's point of view, as well as from the employee's side.

As a St. Leo University magna cum laude graduate, Manresa holds a bachelor's degree in business administration and is currently working on her master's degree in theology.

Leaving behind 20 years of employment in the public sector, Maritza currently owns and manages a business with her husband, Manny. Maritza has two children: Wesley, who is currently attending the University of Florida, and Monica, who is in middle school. Maritza is also a freelance writer, contributing regularly to Factoidz, an online expert advice forum. She authored the recently published book, *How to Open and Operate a Financially Successful Import Export Business.*